After
DIVESTITURE

SUNY Series in Public Administration

Peter W. Colby, editor

After
DIVESTITURE

The Political Economy of
State Telecommunications Regulation

Paul Eric Teske

STATE UNIVERSITY OF NEW YORK PRESS

Published by
State University of New York Press, Albany

©1990 State University of New York

For information, address State University of New York
Press, State University Plaza, N.Y., 12246

Library of Congress Cataloging-in-Publication Data

Teske, Paul Eric.
  After divestiture : the political economy of state
telecommunications regulation / Paul Eric Teske.
    p. cm. — (SUNY series in public administration)
  Includes bibliographical references.
  ISBN 0-7914-0323-8. — ISBN 0-7914-0324-6 (pbk.)
    1. Telecommunication policy—United States—States. 2. Telephone—
Government policy—United States—States. 3. Telecommunication
policy—United States—States—Case studies. 4. Telephone—
Government policy—United States—States—Case studies.   I. Title.
II. Series.
HE7781.T444   1990
384'.068—dc20   89-21851
                                                                          CIP

10 9 8 7 6 5 4 3 2 1

To My Father,

Emil W. Teske

1922 - 1977

CONTENTS

LIST OF TABLES

PREFACE

Many Americans were shocked when AT&T was broken up by a federal government antitrust case in 1982. "If it ain't broke, why fix it?" they asked. AT&T had provided reliable, affordable telephone service to most Americans for more than sixty years. After divestiture, consumers could no longer take for granted inexpensive local rates and convenient, "one-stop" service.

Many scholars have analyzed federal telecommunications policy decisions in the 1980s. Few have tried to explain state choices. Yet state regulators are the nearest government officials to consumers faced with deregulating telecommunications services. This book presents an analysis of U.S. state telecommunications regulatory decisions after the AT&T divestiture. The methodology includes both quantitative analyses and case studies to test theories and to explain state regulatory choices in telecommunications.

On a theoretical level, the analysis in this book is used to test political economy theories of policy choice. Social scientists often disagree about the primary causes of significant changes in public policy, such as the widespread deregulation of American industry over the last decade. Can deregulation be explained using the regulatory theories of the past, or is it a new phenomenon requiring a new theory? Certainly for deregulation to take place, as with regulation, there must be a demand for it in society and a supply of it by government. Interest groups usually provide this demand and government institutions supply the policies. I thus consider both the interest group theory and the institutional theory.

Scholars have analyzed a handful of cases at the federal level to try to explain deregulation. Economists mainly focus on changing technology and economics, and their effect on interest groups that lobby for policies (for example, Becker, 1985), while political scientists more often focus on institutional actors within government and their acceptance of ideas about competition (McCraw, 1984; Derthick and Quirk, 1985).

More cases of deregulation must be analyzed before the essential causes of policy change and the interaction of economic and political factors can be determined. I use state telecommunications regulation

after the AT&T divestiture as a laboratory to test theories of regulatory change. In addition, for the purpose of policy analysis, I answer
questions about U.S. telecommunications policy, especially the different state choices about rate structures and competitive entry.

Chapter 1 examines the history of telecommunications regulation and presents a new angle on the explanation of the divestiture of
AT&T. Chapter 2 presents regulatory theories and integrates the
interest group and institutional views, particularly as they apply to
state regulatory decisions. Chapter 3 presents normative conclusions
about economic pricing, which suggest that local access prices should
be increased and toll prices reduced. It also summarizes the extent to
which this policy has been followed at the federal and state levels.
Chapter 4 analyzes the incidence of changing prices and opening
markets for different interest groups. It finds that large users stand to
gain a great deal from efficient pricing, while a majority of residential
consumers stand to lose from the first-order impacts of changing
prices. Except for rural consumers, however, these losses are not so
large or so regressive, in terms of income, as many analysts have
suggested.

The second half of this book presents the tests of the theories.
Chapter 5 explains the quantitative models and the results of the
regression analysis. I find that variables from institutional theory,
such as legislative party control and regulatory budget, are necessary
to explain state choices and perform better than only interest group
and contextual factors. Chapter 6 explores decision-making in New
Jersey, where the predictions of the models in Chapter 5 are not cor-
rect, and compares New Jersey to its neighboring state, New York,
which followed the quantitative predictions closely. It finds that
bureaucratic expertise is an important element in innovative policy.
Chapter 7, to understand the mechanisms and relationships of
institutional forces, examines regulatory choices in three states that
have made innovative policy choices. It highlights the roles of policy
entrepreneurship and legislative–bureaucratic interaction. Chapter 8
shows how U S West, the most active regulated telecommunications
firm, has used its influence with state regulators, and how institutional factors have mediated U S West's success.

Chapter 9 summarizes my findings and draws general conclusions about theories of regulatory change and about telecommunications policy. Even sophisticated interest group theories are inadequate to explain the variety of state regulatory choices. Since many
groups are active in pressuring regulators, no single group is dominant, and regulators have more autonomy in their decision-making.
As a result, the institutional factors that influence regulators must be
taken into account, and the institutional theory of regulatory policy-
making is supported.

STATE TELECOMMUNICATIONS REGULATION

Why is this book focusing on state regulation, when so much telecommunications activity takes place in Washington, D.C.? State public utility commission regulators were thrust into the limelight in 1984, after playing minor roles in telecommunications regulation for 75 years. They have faced difficult policy choices, compounded by complex economic issues and the interests of several different groups. While much media attention has focused on Washington policymakers, such as former Federal Communications Commission (FCC) Chairman Mark Fowler and Judge Harold Greene, state regulators have emerged collectively as vital decision-makers in the implementation of telephone deregulation. As the *Wall Street Journal* notes: "Although federal regulation gets more attention, state regulation of the Baby Bells currently affects them more strongly" (Roberts, 1987).

Although the divestiture of the local telephone operating companies from AT&T partially resolved some national public policy issues that had been debated for 25 years, it created several new policy problems for all 50 state regulatory agencies. How should states price, and who should be allowed to provide, intrastate telecommunications services? Which services should be deregulated?

Divestiture and the associated telephone deregulation pursued by the FCC helped resolve the issues of interstate long distance competition, customer premise equipment, and switched network interconnection; but it also raised several new issues, including price structures and the extent of competitive entry in various telecommunications services. The FCC has struggled with the pricing issues on the federal level, while Judge Greene and the U.S. Department of Justice have decided most of the competitive questions related to divestiture. States have also faced many decisions about these issues, often while being constrained by federal choices. State public utility commissions have faced decisions about whether to change the historic structure of telephone prices and whether to allow competition with the local telephone companies in the services they provide.

VALUE OF THE STUDY

Five years after divestiture, there is no scholarly consensus on the success of deregulation of the telecommunications industry, compared to general agreement on the success of airline, railroad, and trucking deregulation. Those who seek to understand, influence, and improve government regulation in our society must answer two important questions. The first is the normative question of what constitutes good regulatory policy in promoting efficiency, equity, and technological innovation. The second is why such policies are or are not implemented by government regulatory agencies. While answering the first question is not easy, answering the second can be even more difficult.

The post-divestiture telecommunications environment offers an excellent and rare opportunity to measure the influence of various factors on regulatory outcomes. All 50 states have faced the same types of nonincremental decisions under the same constraints from the federal government, each with a somewhat different scenario of interest groups, contextual variables, and institutional factors. By understanding how these differences affect policy outcomes, we can gain insight into the implementation of regulatory policies.

While political scientists must learn more about policy formulation and implementation at all levels of government, it is particularly significant at the state level. In the 1980s, decisions made at the federal level have increased the responsibilities of state governments. We must determine how well prepared our state governmental structures are to meet these challenges. Case studies of state regulators are relatively rare (see, for example, Joskow, 1972; Anderson, 1981; O'Toole and Montjoy, 1984; Meier, 1988). As state regulatory institutions emerged as important political actors in the energy area in the 1970s and in telecommunications in the 1980s, it is vital to understand their role more fully.

Linking the econometric and case-study approaches provides synergy to this analysis. James Q. Wilson (1985) has noted that "combining the two strategies holds out the prospect for obtaining both the virtues of outcome-oriented, systematic data and the broader, deeper possibilities inherent in carefully worked out comparative case studies. This approach can open the questions that have been neglected in the area of regulatory behavior, namely: what difference does it make how we regulate, and what difference, if any, does it make whether we regulate by one organizational structure or another?" (p. 363). These results suggest that it does make a difference how we regulate telecommunications at the state level.

ACKNOWLEDGMENTS

I could not have written this book without the help of several people. My three dissertation advisers at Princeton University's Woodrow Wilson School provided much help and support on this project. R. Douglas Arnold was especially helpful with his general guidance throughout and his thorough editing. Robert D. Willig helped by sharing his knowledge of economics and the telecommunications industry. Frequent discussions with Peter Van Doren about the nature of political economy and empirical methods led me to several important insights.

I would like to thank the staff of the Woodrow Wilson School for their helpful assistance and administrative support during my graduate studies. I also acknowledge the support of the Olin Foundation, through Princeton University, for the summer of 1987. The Political Science Department at Stony Brook has been very helpful in advancing this research.

The ideas in this book were influenced greatly by related work I have done in telecommunications policy. I thank Linda Garcia and Mark Nadel from the U.S. Congressional Office of Technology Assessment, the late Michael Rice from the Aspen Institute Program in Communications and Society, Heikki Leesment of the New Jersey Board of Public Utilities, and Terry Agriss and Tom Dunleavy of the New York City Office of Energy and Telecommunications. Several others have provided valuable input into this analysis, directly or indirectly, but I would like to acknowledge especially Glenn Richards, Chuck Cameron, Mark Schneider, John Scholz, Howard Scarrow, Nick van de Walle, and Ashok Subramanian.

My mother, Jean Teske, provided helpful support and enthusiasm during this project. Finally, for her support and encouragement I would like to thank Kim Hartman, my wife.

1   Telecommunications Regulatory History

When the U.S. Department of Justice announced the Consent Decree for the divestiture of the local operating companies from AT&T in early 1982, the American telecommunications industry had been regulated by public agencies for over 75 years. For most of that period, industry structure was stable; both federal and state regulation were relatively straightforward, focusing on the rate-of-return on investment to which AT&T and its local operating companies were entitled. For the past 30 years, technological change and federal regulatory choices have gradually shaped the current set of policy issues faced by state and federal regulators. With the 1982 agreement to break up AT&T, these changes accelerated sharply.

In this chapter I examine the history of telecommunications regulation and explain divestiture and federal deregulation with a theoretical framework utilizing interest group and institutional elements. (This framework is developed more generally in Chapter 2.) I also discuss the policy issues that faced federal and state regulators after divestiture. Given this background, the specific state regulatory policy options explained in Chapter 3 and examined in the rest of the book will be anchored in a broader historical contest.

HISTORY

The American telecommunications industry has experienced short periods of competition and longer periods of regulated monopoly, driven by both technological changes and efforts by the firms in the industry. From the outset, inventors competed to develop the new technology. Alexander Graham Bell patented his invention of a telephone on February 17, 1876, only one hour before Elisha Gray, of Western Union, then the dominant telecommunications firm, would have patented a similar invention. A long patent battle ensued before the new Bell Company won a settlement and began to develop the telephone industry with its patent monopoly.

Following the expiration of the patent, from 1884 to 1907 the Bell company and its competitors fought to capture subscribers onto their networks (Brock, 1981). Competition developed in the form of small farmers' cooperatives (some of which still exist today) and larger networks.

In 1907, AT&T initiated its efforts to close the competitive period. Theodore Vail and the Morgan banking interests took over the company and began developing the modern, vertically integrated AT&T, with the explicit goal of becoming a regulated monopoly. Vail saw regulation as a way to stabilize industry profits and to increase his firm's market share. On the federal level, Vail shaped the 1913 Kingsbury Committment, which authorized consolidation of several smaller systems under AT&T. AT&T achieved further consolidation after the First World War. Until 1934, the Interstate Commerce Commission monitored federal telephone issues, prior to the birth of the Federal Communications Commission (FCC).

State telephone regulation also began in 1907, with progressives in New York and Wisconsin establishing the first public utility comissions (PUCs). Most states formed public utility commissions soon afterward. State legislatures gave these commissions the power to prevent monopoly pricing abuses by the rapidly growing electric and telephone companies. Thus, the two-tiered system of telephone regulation that exists today started in 1907.

The 1934 Communications Act authorized continuing federal institutional involvement in telephone regulation by establishing the FCC, thus articulating the goal of universal, affordable telephone service for all Americans. By 1934, AT&T had achieved its goal of becoming the vertically integrated, dominant U.S. telephone company: It controlled 80 percent of U.S. telephones (about the same level as it held in 1982); the only real long distance network in the nation; and Western Electric, which produced all of the equipment for use on the AT&T network (Brock, 1981).

Early Telephone Rate Design

Analysts have debated the question of how to price telephone service since the 1920s. There are two concepts of pricing: board-to-board and station-to-station. Board-to-board pricing followed naturally from the historical development of the network. Local exchanges were constructed first and then linked by long distance connections. Under the board-to-board philosophy, a long distance call is viewed as having only one cost element, from the switchboard of one exchange to the switchboard in another exchange. The U.S. Supreme Court decision in *Smith vs. Illinois Bell* in 1931, however, ruled that because long distance calls require the use of local exchanges on both ends for connection, toll prices must include a part of the cost of the local exchange. This decision supported the station-to-station view of costs, in which the cost of a long distance call is traced from telephone to telephone.

After this decision, regulators began to develop the practice of "separations and settlements" to direct revenues to the proper cost jurisdictions for rate-making purposes. The Federal Communications Commission, state regulators, and AT&T adopted the first major separations and settlements plan in 1943 to direct AT&T toll revenues to Bell companies in different states and to non-Bell, independent local telephone companies. The specific methodology for this practice changed incrementally over the next fifteen years. Generally, however, telephone issues remained quiet in the 1940s and 1950s, as advancing technology reduced costs for both local and toll service, and regulators faced few pricing problems. While this stable environment continued through the 1970s for state regulators, technological change, particularly the development of microwave communications, began to cloud the horizon for federal regulators.

Telephone Deregulation Events

In 1959 the FCC made its "Above 890" decision that allowed companies other than AT&T to provide services at those microwave frequencies. This decision did not immediately alter the telephone regulatory environment, but it was the first major regulatory step toward competition with the switched, public network. Along with other FCC decisions in the 1960s and 1970s, it set the stage for fundamental change in the industry. Microwave Communications Inc. (MCI) would use the "Above 890" decision to apply to serve private parties in Chicago and St. Louis just four years later.

In 1966 the FCC began its "Computer Inquiry I" (Computer Inquiry III was concluded in 1987) to consider the implications of merging technologies in computers and telecommunications. The commissioners realized that it would become increasingly difficult to encourage the unregulated development of computer services while at the same time regulating the telephone system upon which computer communication relies. In its 1968 "CarterPhone" decision, the FCC ruled that non-AT&T equipment could be attached to the network without causing damage. The FCC reacted to the convergence of computer and telecommunications technology by relaxing regulation somewhat.

In 1969 the FCC authorized MCI, after six years of consideration, to operate private microwave service between Chicago and St. Louis.

The FCC's 1970 "Specialized Common Carrier" decision allowed private microwave communication by other firms as well. AT&T argued unsuccessfully that these decisions encouraged other firms to "skim the cream" off the most profitable long distance routes. Since the FCC required AT&T to serve all routes, including the less profitable ones, AT&T argued that this competition, though limited, could destroy the existing practice of averaging prices by distance across routes with very different costs.

In 1971, the federal regulators, AT&T, other local telephone companies, and state regulators established the Ozark Plan for separations and settlements. This cost allocation methodology changed the existing practice by shifting more of the recovery of non-traffic-sensitive access costs from local to toll rates.[1] Regulators found such a shift in cost allocation politically palatable because technology was driving toll costs down, while local access costs were no longer falling. The Ozark Plan utilized an elaborate but economically arbitrary system of apportioning costs.[2] The Ozark Plan allocated an increasing amount of non-traffic-sensitive costs to interstate tolls from 1971 to 1984 (Congressional Budget Office, 1984).

Largely as a result of the Ozark Plan, average monthly local rates fell from $12.14 in 1970 to $8.61 by 1980, in constant 1980 dollars. The increase in local telephone rates from 1967 to 1984 was the fourth lowest among all goods surveyed in the Consumer Price Index, growing only 114 percent while the CPI increased 311 percent.

In a separate chain of events, in 1974 the U.S. Department of Justice (DOJ) initiated an antitrust suit against AT&T on the grounds of conspiracy to monopolize.[3] This suit combined several complaints about AT&T purchasing and pricing policies. The Department of Justice's main goal was the separation of Western Electric, the manufacturing subsidiary, from AT&T, but as limited competition appeared in long distance markets, government lawyers also sought separation of the local operating companies from the long distance operation. The suit was settled in the 1982 Consent Decree.

Throughout the eight-year period of the antitrust suit, advancing technology forced the FCC to make further decisions about competition in telecommunications. In 1975, the ever-aggressive MCI petitioned for approval of an interconnected, switched network service called "Execunet." The FCC barred Execunet on the grounds that it was not a private line service allowable under the 1970 "Specialized Common Carrier" decision. Upon appeal, in 1978 the D.C. District Appeals Court refused to uphold the FCC decision. The court did not disagree with the FCC but held that the FCC had not presented adequate evidence of its position that interconnection would harm the network. Between 1975 and 1978, however, the FCC accepted a more pro-competitive view of the industry and chose not to provide further evidence but to let the court's decision stand. This decision not to try to win the Execunet appeal was the major turning point in the FCC's stand on competition. Some have argued that this decision was as significant in telecommunications deregulation as divestiture.

Faced with these assaults on the competitive and antitrust fronts, AT&T lobbied heavily in Congress for an updated version of the 1934 Communications Act that would protect their position. AT&T argued that competition would take away revenues by "skimming the cream," that is, ending the subsidy to basic local service and threatening universal service. They failed to persuade Congress.[4]

DIVESTITURE

On January 8, 1982, after eight years of the antitrust case, AT&T signed a Consent Decree to divest itself of its local operating companies. The actual divestiture was slated for January 1, 1984, to allow adequate time for development of a plan to split up the network and management assets of the world's largest corporation. The 22 Bell Operating Companies (BOCs) were placed into seven new regional holding companies (RHCs), or "Baby Bells." AT&T kept its long distance network, its manufacturing facilities (Western Electric), and its research arm (Bell Labs). The basic theory was that competition had developed in long distance and equipment markets, and that one of the competitors (AT&T) should not control the "bottleneck" facilities of the local networks.

The BOC local networks were viewed as natural monopolies that should continue to be regulated at the state level. To prevent a repeat at the RHC-level of the incentives that caused the AT&T antitrust suit, the Modified Final Judgment of the Consent Decree prevented the RHCs from entering related telecommunications markets for several years, including equipment manufacturing, information services, and long distance service.[5] States were cordoned off into local access and transport areas (LATAs), roughly corresponding to metropolitan areas or area codes.[6] The Consent Decree gave the BOCs the right to complete calls within LATAs, but did not allow them to carry traffic across LATAs.

Divestiture opened interstate calls to competition, under the FCC's regulatory authority. State regulators were given the option of allowing competition with AT&T for intrastate interLATA calls and it was expected that this would happen under the theory of the case. Similarly, states had authority to allow or prohibit intraLATA competition with the BOCs, although this was perceived as a step for the future.

Explaining Divestiture

Since the discipline of political science takes its surname from using a scientific methodology to understand probabilistic tendencies, regulatory scholars should not feel compelled to explain every single political event. The march of history is probabilistic; on average, one out of every ten events with 0.1 probability of occuring actually does take place. Scholars often try to explain these events retrospectively as if they had to have happened. While we should be aware of probabilities, when the largest corporation in the world, providing the best telephone service to the country with the largest economy in the world, is broken up by the government, as AT&T was in 1982, we must attempt a thorough explanation. And yet, eight years later, we do not have an adequate explanation for the most significant of a series of choices leading to the partial deregulation of the U.S. telecommunications industry.

The deregulation phenomenon cannot itself be considered a surprise as many other U.S. industries and the telecommunications industries of Britain and Japan had been deregulated (although Britain and Japan followed the U.S. lead to some degree). Divestiture itself, however, was a surprise. As Crandall (1988, p. 324) notes: "The major event in the telephone industry has not been deregulation, but divestiture." Furthermore, when the main results six years after divesture include a change from a positive to a negative trade balance in telecommunications equipment, only two real nationwide long distance competitors, a seeming glut of long distance, optical fiber capacity, higher telephone bills for a majority of Americans, and general citizen dissatisfaction with the breakup, we must ask why.

Scholars offer a structural theory of how AT&T, the most powerful force, "won by losing" (MacAvoy and Robinson, 1983), suggesting that AT&T opportunistically shed the slow-growth local exchanges for the right to enter high-growth computer information markets. We are also offered a journalistic account of the mistakes, misunderstandings, and accidents that fueled the antitrust case that directly broke up AT&T, the 0.1 probability description (Coll, 1986). Derthick and Quirk (1985) provide a general explanation of deregulation, using airlines, trucking, and telecommunications as cases, focusing on the "politics of ideas" and the government's accepting economic concepts of competition. They readily admit, however, that these ideas were far less clear in telecommunications than in the other areas. Indeed, economic disagreement still abounds over the basic natural monopoly issues in 1990. Temin (1987), writing the official AT&T history, argues that a change in government ideology favoring competition was more important than technological change or the specific legal issues of the antitrust case. Knott and Hammond (1988) focus on the instability of cartel and monopoly regimes, even those managed by government, but they admit that this explanation also fits other industries better than telecommunications. Other accounts, including those of von Auw (1983) and Horwitz (1989), also do not provide completely satisfactory explanations of the political economy of divestiture and federal telecommunications deregulation. Stone (1989) correctly adds the role of other firms and industries opposed to AT&T to the interest group environment.

An adequate theory must take account of the driving forces behind three strains of change, all of which were probably understood at the time by only a few principals, such as AT&T top management. The AT&T divestiture is an example of independent, incremental decision-making in multiple arenas that led to an outcome few could have predicted. No single public institution made all of the policy choices. Congress could have made explicit and comprehensive policy choices, but chose instead to avoid legislating.

Action on three separate fronts—the Ozark Plan, the FCC's decision to allow competition, and the Department of Justice suit—combined with the inability of AT&T to reverse this momentum in Congress and led to divestiture. The industry and its federal and state regulators decided on the Ozark Plan because it allowed shifting of revenue requirements from local service, where technology was relatively stagnant, to toll, where technology was driving costs down. As large users developed other options for toll calling, they threatened the sustainability of this approach. The FCC was gradually moving towards a pro-competitive posture, and clearly the turning point was its choice not to try to overturn the "Execunet" court decision. At the same time, the Justice Department was pursuing its own case to prove that AT&T unfairly used monopolistic purchasing and pricing practices.

Political Economy Explanation

A political economy theory of deregulation has both a supply and a demand side, as Stigler (1971) postulated for theories of economic regulation. Of course, Stigler and most economists do not consider the supply side in any detail. Interest groups represent the demand side, and their influence in divestiture and in federal telecommunications deregulation has been underappreciated, except by Stone (1989). Government institutions represent the supply side; the aforementioned telecommunications scholars have been fairly successful in explaining and chronicling their ideas and interactions in telecommunications deregulation.

Interest Groups and Divestiture

To understand political influence from interest group preferences to policy outcomes, we must consider the powerful interest groups in the telecommunications arena, and the extent to which the apparent economic consequences of divestiture and deregulation as of 1990 could have been anticipated or are surprises. The constellation of interests in telecommunications regulation at the time of divestiture included AT&T, its unionized employees (e.g., CWA, IBEW), actual competitors (e.g., MCI), small business and residential consumers, large business users of telecommunications services, and equipment suppliers and potential competitors (e.g., IBM). I will consider, in turn, their preferences and resulting outcomes.

AT&T, in its pre-divestiture form, had tremendous political clout, with about one million employees and three million stockholders. Yet they failed to persuade Congress to halt the FCC's competitive trend in the way they desired (von Auw, 1983; Derthick and Quirk, 1985; Coll, 1986; Temin, 1987). Still, since divestiture was so complicated, many assume that powerful AT&T must have walked away with the best deal. Today, most analysts dismiss the AT&T "won by losing" explanation by pointing to their financial losses in computer markets, their loss of long distance market share, the thousands of employees laid off, and reduced stockholder earnings, all in contrast to the surprising financial health of the regional holding companies and Bell Operating Companies created and spun off, respectively, in the divestiture. The more fundamental critique of the "won by losing" theory is that AT&T fought as hard as possible against divestiture for a decade, until top management shifted its view just prior to the January 8, 1982 Consent Decree. AT&T tried and failed to persuade Congress to reverse the thrust of telecommunications policy change. Certainly AT&T tried to strike a good deal in the Consent Decree once it had decided internally to divest, but getting the best out of a bad situation is not equivalent to orchestrating a process to achieve everything one wants.

No one can argue that the RHCs forced divestiture as they did not exist prior to the event (a situation that led to unsuccessful lawsuits about the court's right to regulate them under the MFJ). Their financial success since their birth in 1984 has been a surprise to almost everyone, including Wall Street stock analysts. Their average stock return was twice that of AT&T between 1984 and 1988 (Crandall, 1988).

But what about the unionized employees of AT&T? In many other nations, telecommunications services are delivered by a state-run Postal, Telegraph, and Telephone (PTT) enterprise, and long distance profits subsidize postal services. In several countries, such as

West Germany, the PTT is the largest employer and its unionized workers have significant clout, particularly in opposing privatization. In the United States, however, it is difficult to argue that unionized AT&T employees got what they wanted from recent telecommunications policy. While relative wages in the telecommunications have not been reduced greatly since 1984 (Hendricks, 1989), thousands of employees have been laid off from AT&T and the RHCs, and new competitors often are not unionized. Unionized telecommunications employees opposed deregulation and lost.

One obvious and populist possibility is that direct competitors won the game. Through the development of an amazingly brilliant and persistant strategy, Bill McGowan became MCI's David to the Goliath of AT&T (see Kahaner, 1987). Yet, it can also be argued that MCI's early success was a function of both regulatory distortions in pricing, which allowed MCI to "cream-skim," and regulatory limits on the responses of AT&T to MCI's competitive thrusts. MCI would not have succeeded without the FCC's help. As subsequent FCC policy after divestiture moved toward the proverbial "level playing field," MCI, US Sprint, and the few other remaining facilities-based competitors have borne financial losses and their viability as separate entities in the world of optical fiber capacity surplus remains in some doubt. By 1988, they favored freeing AT&T from rate-of-return regulation in the hope that AT&T prices would not be reduced further and they could profit under a pricing umbrella. Clearly MCI won many battles in the 1970s, but may have lost some in the 1980s. Did MCI partly lose by winning?

Deregulation in the banking, airlines, and trucking industries is often described as the amazing victory of widely dispersed consumers over concentrated industry interests (Wilson, 1980; Derthick and Quirk, 1985). With divestiture and subsequent pricing policies, while it is clear that consumers' surplus will increase in the aggregate, the median residential consumer will not gain from the first-order impacts (see Chapter 4 for details). Survey evidence strongly supports the economic evidence that residential consumers do not view themselves as winners from divestiture. Chapter 4 shows the dissatisfaction with divestiture that consumers still held in 1988, in contrast to widespread satisfaction with telephone service before 1984. Thus, residential consumers did not push for or do well by divestiture.

Are we then left with only the accident theory (Coll, 1986) combined with MCI's valient effort (Kahaner, 1987)? No, because there are other important interest groups that played a significant role: large business users of telecommunications services and potential competitors, including equipment suppliers. The first group are specialized consumers, particularly, although not exclusively, large white-collar service firms. The second includes firms that wanted to compete in markets monopolized by AT&T, including equipment providers that were shut out of the vertically integrated AT&T purchasing from Western Electric, and computer companies, most prominently IBM. Together these firms provided a potent coalition opposed to AT&T's monopoly control over telecommunications services.

The importance of large business users is a result of the skewed demand for toll calls; about 1 percent of all business locations generate more than 25 percent of all toll revenues. Evidence suggests that computer service firms, financial firms, and airlines (all unregulated or recently deregulated industries) are among the largest users. These firms take telecommunications seriously and consider it not only as an input cost of production, but as a strategic asset; Manufacturers Hanover Bank, for example, employs over 300 telecommunications workers, even excluding those devoted to data processing or automatic teller machines.

Large users are organized into several political action groups, including (1) the Committee of Corporate Telecommunications Users (CCTU), made up of large U.S. companies; (2) the International Communications Association (ICA), representing 550 of the world's largest users, each of which spends at least $1 million per year on telecommunications; (3) the New York Clearinghouse Association, composed of 12 New York City—headquartered banks, including six of the ten largest in the United States; (4) the Utilities Telecommunications Council, representing 2,000 electric, gas, water and steam utilities; and (5) the Association of Data Communications Users, representing 175 high-use corporations and institutions, including banks, insurance companies, universities, and manufacturers (General Accounting Office Report, 1986). These groups participate in federal and state regulatory proceedings and hold the additional advantage of being able to establish their own networks to "bypass" the public, switched network for their own internal traffic. Quirk (1988) argues that these groups did not participate actively in the legal case leading to divestiture; but active political participation, which did come later for some of these organizations, is not always necessary for firms with options and implicit political power (Lindblom, 1977). Furthermore, Stone (1989) shows that IBM, the American Petroleum Institute, Westinghouse, and others have participated actively in telecommunications regulatory proceedings for several decades.

As previously noted, MCI was a potential competitor to AT&T in the 1960s, but it forced legal action and became an actual competitor by the late 1970s. Other potential competitors included IBM and equipment providers who sought to sell their goods for use on the

AT&T network, but had little chance when the AT&T subsidiary, Western Electric, produced such equipment. Equipment providers (although not always American firms) have been large winners from divestiture: "roughly half of all new telephone investment is being undertaken by entities other than the local or long-distance companies" (Crandall, 1988, p. 326). Aronson and Cowhey (1988) note that "large users, international service providers, and large electronic firms ... are the center of the telecommunications reform coalition" (p. 266).

With the technological feasibility of bypass, the distinction between large users and potential competitors blurs somewhat (see Irwin, 1984). From the start MCI has been one of the largest customers of AT&T, by leasing capacity, because until the late 1980s MCI did not have a true national network. And, conversely, after divestiture, AT&T became the largest customer by far of each RHC, because of the fees paid for access to their local networks, which represented at least 50 percent of AT&T post-divestiture long distance costs.

While Noll and Owen (1983) note that the "Association of Potential Competitors" is not listed in the Washington, D.C. telephone book, it is not true that such players have or had little clout in divestiture. IBM was one of the crucial supporters of changes in telecommunications. Ironically, on the same day that the AT&T Consent Decree was signed, a major antitrust suit against IBM was dropped, leading some pundits to suggest that the two decisions had been switched in the mail. As Stone (1989) notes: "The computer industry (including IBM) was partly responsible for changes in telecommunications policy [from 1969-1982]." (p. 239).

IBM, seeing connectivity and distributed data processing as the future in computer markets, supported a Charles River Associates/ Harvard University study of telecommunications that, despite admittedly ambiguous economic evidence, advocated competition in long distance carriage (Meyer et al., 1980). After 1982, IBM purchased a substantial stake in several telecommunications firms, including MCI, Rolm, an equipment provider, and a shared tenant services (STS) provider, which placed them squarely in every major telecommunications market. After 1984, 10 percent of IBM's substantial revenues came from telecommunications-related businesses. Still, IBM's "strategy is not to become a big player in ordinary long-distance, but to protect its basic computer business" (Kirkland, 1984, p. 54).

More recently, IBM developed the concept of Open Network Architecture (ONA) as a way to end the local monopoly of the RHCs, a spinoff of its "systems network architecture" developed in the 1970s. ONA, while not fully developed, has generated a significant amount of interest and controversy. IBM is also active in debates about Integrated Services Digital Networks (ISDN), because the more "intelligence" that is built into such telecommunications networks, the less computer support that is needed at the nodes of the network. Whether IBM's involvement in telecommunications is viewed as more offensive or defensive, its significance has often been overlooked. While popular business publications view the AT&T–IBM competition largely from the perspective of AT&T being allowed to enter IBM's computer territory after divestiture (generally a financial failure for AT&T as of 1990), the opposite invasion may have been a more significant influence leading to divestiture.

Thus, large users and potential competitors played a crucial role in telecommunications deregulation and in divestiture, with IBM, not MCI or AT&T, as perhaps the most significant winner of the era. These user/competitor firms held important implicit political levers of a large employment base, high-tech status, vital research and development capabilities, spearheading U.S. competition abroad, and the ability to leave the shared network, in addition to their explicit political lobbying strength.

The United States is not the only country in which these actors played critical roles. The Keidenran in Japan, a tightly knit organization of the largest firms, provided strong and effective pressure for competition in telecommunications services and equipment (Harris, 1988). Aronson and Cowhey (1988) note that it is no concidence that the three countries that have most substantially liberalized or deregulated their telecommunications industries, the United States, Britain, and Japan, all have cities vying for world financial leadership—New York, London, and Tokyo.

Interests, Ideas, and Institutions

While these competitors and large users are extremely important in explaining deregulation and divestiture, they only represent the demand side of the picture. Ideas about competition and important institutional decisions, particularly those made by the FCC in the 1970s, must be included in the explanation. The role of deregulatory economic ideas cannot be dismissed. Deregulation was on the minds of decision-makers because of its seeming success in other industries and because of technological changes in telecommunications.

However, ideas shaped by technological and market changes still need a substantial coalition of political support for their development. The theory supported here is that technological change shaped ideas about competition and deregulation in the convergence of data processing and telecommunications. Actual and potential competitors, especially MCI, IBM, and equipment providers, combined with large users, especially financial firms, to pressure decision-makers to recognize these changes. These interests embodied and lobbied for the ideas; they were the sources of economic and political pressure to eliminate the deadweight losses that Becker (1983, 1985) and Keeler (1984) identify as potential counterbalances to inefficient economic regulation.

In contrast to the large users, small consumers inevitably faced losses after divestiture as the maintenance of a cross-subsidy became less tenable in competitive markets. Lumping all consumers or users of a product together makes no more sense for political scientists and policy analysts studying interest group activity in regulation than it does for business marketing specialists trying to sell their products or for political campaign strategists trying to stimulate votes.

POLICY ISSUES AFTER DIVESTITURE

Divestiture was the focal point of monumental changes in the telecommunications industry. For business scholars the breakup of the world's largest corporation raised issues of management, strategic planning, and international competitiveness in corporate transition. For economists, divestiture launched a brave new era in competitive market structure despite substantial disagreement on answers to the monopoly and competition questions. For political scientists, it posed the important question of how bureaucracies would make decisions in the transition to a more competitive era.

Divestiture did solve several problems plaguing regulators. Interstate long distance competition became the federal policy, although the methods and degree of regulating AT&T have continued to be very controversial. The FCC did establish rules to allow nondiscriminatory access to the local networks for long distance carriers and set up a schedule for BOC implementation of "equal access."[7] Many new carriers appeared and emerging carriers expanded to build national networks, at least two of which seem poised to survive into the 1990s. Divestiture effectively opened the telecommunications equipment market to competition, as the BOCs are no longer wedded to Western Electric. New equipment firms, both domestic and foreign, emerged ready to take advantage of these opportunities. Crandall (1988) notes that the equipment markets have become the most competitive telecommunications markets after divestiture.

While divestiture established clear policy directions in interstate long distance and in equipment markets, it raised additional policy problems for federal and state regulators. The FCC has continued to struggle with the question of how to phase in long distance competition in a market with a dominant carrier holding a 50 to 70 percent market share. Judge Greene and the Justice Department have continued to decide whether and how to give the Baby Bells waivers to expand into new services. State regulators have encountered a host of new issues regarding rate structures and competitive entry. The lack of clear rules about federal and state jurisdiction has made all of these problems more difficult (Noam, 1983; Maher, 1985), and Congress has continued to avoid explicit policy making.

After divestiture, the 50 state regulatory commissions have all faced many new issues requiring quick resolution. In the area of pricing, state regulators have ruled on end-user access pricing, long distance–carrier access pricing, possible deaveraging of toll and local rates, local measured service, and depreciation issues. State regulators have needed to develop an appropriate competitive/regulatory mix on such issues as intrastate interLATA competition, intraLATA competition, Centrex policy, and new business services.

Proper pricing of telecommunications services is a difficult task. The tariff structure existing in most states in 1984 was an artifact of AT&T policies, some recent competitive pressures, and numerous cross-subsidies that regulators found convenient. While the FCC decided on methods to shift non-traffic-sensitive access costs from toll usage to end-users, state regulators have faced decisions about whether and how to follow suit. Furthermore, many states had priced local service on a "value of service" basis in which subscribers who could reach fewer other subscribers on the local exchange paid less than those who could reach more people with a local call. The value of service pricing method yielded the opposite results from cost-based pricing, in which rates would be lower for subscribers in more dense areas. Whether and how to change these pricing philosophies has presented serious problems for state regulators.

At the same time that cross-subsidies were threatened, regulators also have faced the problem of underdepreciated assets, with an attendant intergenerational subsidy. In the monopoly environment, installation of telephone service and subscriber premise inside wire was capitalized over twenty years. Other equipment was depreciated according to long schedules to keep current prices low. Depreciation schedules are not vital to firms in a monopoly environment because costs can be spread over time. In a competitive industry, however, depreciation must reflect economic costs so that investment decisions can be made properly.

After divestiture, the FCC changed accounting rules to expense on a current basis these formerly capitalized costs and to gradually eliminate the existing depreciation reserve deficiency. At the state level, regulators have faced similar decisions about depreciation practices.[8] The recovery, or write-off, of past underdepreciation is a purely distributive political issue in that economic theory does not really care who pays for them—subscribers or shareholders—because they are uneconomic sunk costs that do not affect decisions at the margin but do remain on the books. Therefore, state regulators have had more discretion on this issue. Any increase in depreciation recovery, however, past or future, only drives current rates up further.

The competitive issues have aligned closely with the pricing issues. Allowing intrastate interLATA competition means developing intrastate carrier access charges to either mirror the FCC's interstate charges or reflect other concerns. Authorizing intraLATA competition means subjecting the BOCs to competitive rates possibly before their rates are cost-based, a major handicap. New pricing policies for Centrex have been necessary to allow the service to compete with private branch exchanges (PBXs) and prevent stranded BOC equipment.[9]

CONCLUSIONS

The history of telecommunications is more complicated than the surface appearance of years of AT&T natural monopoly followed by an abrupt antitrust decision breaking up the company's vertically integrated structure. Interested parties have debated the pricing of long distance and local services for over sixty years. Divestiture, while certainly the focal point of changes in telecommunications, was by no means the only important choice made over the past thirty years. A complete understanding of divestiture and related federal deregulation requires analysis of interest group demands for change and their interaction with institutional ideas.

In the next chapter I discuss the theoretical issues involved in the interest group and institutional perspectives, leading to their application in explaining cross-state variation in regulatory choices.

2

Political Economic
Theories of Deregulation

After the divestiture of AT&T, state regulators of telecommunications services faced two fundamental questions. First, how should local service be priced, given that large business users threatened to leave the regulated network because toll prices were well above marginal costs? Second, given that many of the services provided by the local operating companies, including intraLATA long distance transmission, may not have been natural monopolies, should free entry be allowed into these markets? States responded differently to these two questions. Some states altered prices to reflect marginal costs while others maintained pricing systems filled with cross-subsidies. Some states encouraged intraLATA competition while others continued to restrict entry totally.

Scholars who study regulatory policy offer several classes of explanation for government decision making. Chapter 1 illustrated how these theories explain federal choices leading to divestiture. In this chapter I describe these theories more fully and relate them to the state telecommunications environment. Two broad explanations are possible. Advocates of the first argue that interest groups and contextual variables dominate outcomes and that governmental institutions are irrelevant. Scholars supporting the second, the institutional theory, stress the importance of governmental institutional structure, regulators, and their relationship with legislators.

THEORIES OF REGULATION AND DEREGULATION

Some scholars believe that regulatory behavior is governed largely by the preferences of interest groups, which are partly shaped by economic and technological contextual factors. In extreme versions of this theory advanced by economists, the design of regulatory institutions, and the identities and beliefs of regulators are of no consequence (Stigler, 1971; Peltzman, 1976). Rent-seeking interest groups will dominate outcomes. This concept of "regulatory capture" is not new. Political scientists have long recognized that regulated firms have been able to use informational advantages in the regulatory process itself and other channels of political influence, including appointments and campaign contributions, to get what they want

(Huntington, 1952; Bernstein, 1955; Lowi, 1969). In less dogmatic versions of this theory, interest groups are viewed as playing an important role but not completely overwhelming other factors (Noll and Owen, 1983; Moe, 1985).

Other scholars believe that bureaucratic factors, political entrepreneurs, and the acceptance of ideas about regulation—sometimes of the "public interest" variety—, account for changes in regulatory behavior more than interest group pressure (Wilson, 1980; Quirk, 1981; McCraw, 1984; Derthick and Quirk, 1985; Meier, 1988). Regulatory policy is not simply a function of net interest group pressure. Deregulation, according to this view, is the dispersal of gains, or economic rents, from concentrated interest groups back to the broad mass of consumers. Political entrepreneurs and government bureaucrats have developed an understanding of the positive and normative economics of regulation and acted appropriately, recognizing a failure of the old public interest theories and the need for more competition to aid consumers (McCraw, 1984; Derthick and Quirk, 1985). Economic ideas about deregulation gained support at a time when politicians and bureaucrats became finely attuned to the supposed macroeconomic consequences of microeconomic policies; these macroeconomic concerns focused on inflation in the mid-1970s to early 1980s and on the international competitiveness of American industry after trade issues and deficits became salient in the early 1980s.

Advocates of interest group theories grant that political entrepreneurs are needed to help push and support deregulation, but argue that regulatory change is still best explained by rent-seeking (Braeutigam and Owen, 1978; Ackerman and Hassler, 1981). Their argument is often tautological; as changes in regulation almost always have positive or negative effects for different groups (see Leone, 1986), policy implementation is always a function more of effective interest group lobbying than good public interest–oriented policy.

To describe an integrated political economic theory of deregulation, it is necessary to borrow a few concepts from both economics and political science. As in economic theories of regulation, there is a demand for and a supply of deregulation. Demand is embodied in interest groups, while supply results from institutional decisions, although not simply as a response to the sum of interest group pressure. As with descriptions of inflation in macroeconomic theories, deregulatory policies may be largely of the "demand-pull" or "supply-push" varieties, or a combination of both.

Interest Groups

Interest group and rent-seeking theories of policy outcomes argue that firms and citizens use the political system to gain wealth and income not obtainable through ordinary market relationships. Group success in obtaining favorable policy outcomes varies according to their control over bureaucratic and electoral resources. Political scientists have long examined governmental decisions in light of interest group pressure. Much controversy has centered on whether interest group pressure comes from a variety of sources, in a pluralist fashion, or whether a few powerful groups continually dominate outcomes.

In past regulatory issues, it is apparent that regulated firms often held most of the control over government policy. No countervailing force against the regulated firms was sustained; general political enthusiasm and citizen interest may have been present at the establishment of the regulatory agency, but years of slow, technical proceedings led to apathy. Yet, while interest group capture theory is compelling, and perhaps an appropriate description of American regulation after World War II, many political scientists argue that its assumptions are not fully accurate (Wilson, 1974; Quirk, 1981; Meier, 1988). The Federal Communications Commission, for example, clearly was not captured by AT&T in the 1970s.

George Stigler and the so-called Chicago School (Stigler 1971; Posner 1971, 1974; Peltzman 1976) argue that the original decision to begin regulation is frequently promoted by the firms themselves, although wrapped in a package labeled "public interest." They demand regulation to prevent competitive entry, and politicians supply it in return for votes and contributions. This type of rent-seeking activity by firms is often commingled with plausible public interest policy goals (e.g., retaining the AT&T monopoly and encouraging universal service), which makes the importance of the private interest components difficult to detect. AT&T did advance the regulated monopoly concept in the early part of this century (Brock, 1981), but the theory of complete business exploitation of the regulatory process is no longer relevant in telecommunications or most other industries today.

A quasi-pluralist theory of interest group pressure in regulatory and deregulatory policy seems more appropriate today, and may have been in the past as well. Bauer, Pool, and Dexter (1963) pointed out over 25 years ago that politicians have scope to bring other factors, including their personal ideology, into their decisions because many firms pressure them, in different ways. In telecommunications in the 1980s, several incumbent firms, potential and actual competitors, large users of telecommunications services, unionized employees, and small consumers all held interests in regulatory decisions and lobbied to achieve their objectives. Some scholars try to model the pluralist input process in a game-theoretic context (see, for example, Sharkey,

1983) or as an "ecology of games" (Long, 1958; Dutton, 1987). For example, the FCC, state regulators, AT&T, and residential consumers formed a stable, winning coalition in telecommunications regulation for many years; this stability ended when MCI, IBM, large users, the U.S. Department of Justice, and competitive technology entered the telecommunications regulatory arena (see Chapter 1). The FCC opted out of the original coalition and it unraveled, leaving state regulators and residential consumers to try to maintain the status quo.

By relating interest group preferences to policy outcomes we can infer influence (Nagel, 1975). With powerful interest groups on both sides of the main issues, no one interest group can be completely dominant. The pressure now comes in a form that approaches pluralism. Some groups have more resources and more influence, however, so that the pressure is a function of the strength of interested groups as well as the constellation of interests. Yet, in the telecommunications policy debates in the 1980s, the resources available to the various interested groups were more equal than in many other policy arenas. While some concentrated groups held levers in favor of changes in price structure, other business groups were opposed, along with the interests of residential consumers (who are voters).

Sophisticated theories of interest group behavior go beyond a simple determination of group support or opposition; they argue that, holding other factors constant, the resources devoted to a political struggle by interest groups will be proportional to the flows of income at stake in the struggle (Kalt, 1981). Thus, contextual economic variables must be considered. The important contextual factors in telecommunications are the interstate flow of cross-subsidies and the economics of access to the network. States receiving cross-subsidies may be more likely to favor the status quo in decisions about price structures and competitive entry. States with higher average access costs may be more likely to change prices and to oppose competitive entry.

If these differing contextual variables completely explain different regulatory outcomes, then none of the political influence models of regulatory decision making are verified. Regulators may simply be reacting to economic and technological factors that differ across the states. While the interest group and contextual theories partly attempt to distinguish political and economic influences, these influences are not truly separate. Large users hold both political clout and the latent economic (contextual) threat of bypass. Similarly, entrenched cable television firms hold both potential political and economic strength. The NECA interstate subsidy can be interpreted as the influence of different states as interest groups in the interstate rate-making process. The economics of access to the network are more nearly pure contextual factors; even access costs, however, capture elements of the threat to rural political interests in a state. The over-lap of interest group and contextual factors is not a problem for the theory; it simply means that contextual factors should be considered along with interest groups as political economic influences outside of the institutional structures of regulation.

Institutional Theory

The main alternative theory to interest groups is the institutional theory, which holds that governmental actors can act independently of net interest group pressure. Political scientists have used this theory in recent years to "bring the state back in" (see, for example, Nordlinger, 1981). To understand why such a theory is important in regulation, we must turn to the interaction of interest groups and institutional actors.

Interest group theorists argue that affected groups lobby for regulatory changes favoring them, both in the legislative and bureaucratic arenas. Their effectiveness in overcoming free-rider organizational problems is generally a function of group size and per capita stakes (Olson, 1965). Exogenous forces, such as technological change, and endogenous institutional choices, such as government funding of consumer advocates, can change the constellation of interest groups over time. Economic theories of interest group pressure do not argue that one and only one interest group will capture regulators, but that a balance of interests will determine policy. What Stigler and many followers have done that political scientists should disagree with is to treat government as a simple "cash register of interests."[1]

In many current regulatory battles, including telecommunications, the interest group environment approaches a crude form of pluralism. Many interest groups compete for influence; they are not all of equal strength and influence, but they are all players in the game. When so many interest groups pressure regulators, complete capture by any one is unlikely. Regulators must balance the political and economic costs and benefits of supporting one group or another. As a result, when the interest group coalitions near a rough equilibrium in strength, regulators have scope to bring other factors into their decisions, including elements of institutional structure (to whom they are most directly accountable), their own attitudes or ideology, advice from their staff, and the oversight of legislative actors.

Those who do not find the institutional theory persuasive argue that such structures of "the state" and the attitudes of key actors are likely to be endogenous to other factors in a state, including the balance of interest group power. They contend that these interests are powerful enough to see that favorable institutions are established and that commissioners are appointed who are inclined towards their positions. This argument, when simply asserted, appears tautological. State telecommunications regulatory structures do not seem endogenous to post-divestiture telecommunications interest groups. Regulatory structures were established under an entirely different era of regulation, that of the Bell system monopoly, when the constellation of interests differed greatly. The structures pre-date the abrupt changes in the telecommunications environment caused by the federally mandated divestiture, and these structures have not changed substantially after the exogenous shock of divestiture. Furthermore, these same bureaucracies regulate several other policy areas upon which the set of important interests differs widely. To which interests are these structures endogenous? If institutions are completely endogenous, how was the FCC able to oppose the most powerful interest in telecommunications, AT&T, in the 1970s?

Endogeneity also involves a time dimension. Variables that may be endogenous in a system of equations can be considered predetermined for the purposes of a short time-period analysis (Kmenta, 1986). It depends on the question one asks. Given that these institutional factors are in place, do they have an impact on policy choices? What determines these structures is a second question, the answer to which *may* also reveal that similar causes (unfortunately, often unmeasured or unmeasurable) influence both the institutional factors and the ultimate policy choices of interest. If so, one may be attributing causation to a intervening, endogenous variable.

A verifying test of this argument would establish that any seeming correlation in empirical analysis between these bureaucratic variables and decision-making is spurious, and caused by the preferences of interest groups or other exogenous factors. Therefore, in the quantitative analysis, I will compare one-stage regression results with two-stage results that treat appropriate institutional factors as endogenous, to perform this test.

Defining institutional theory precisely is difficult, in part because political scientists have not yet agreed on exactly what defines institutions. Clearly, they are originally formed as outputs of competing political coalitions and are shaped by both winning and losing sides. Over time, it would be surprising if institutions did not develop a "life of their own," using their own resources, and the insulation originally given them by the winning coalition to deal with future political uncertainty (Moe, 1989). Thus, institutions can be seen as a mix of interest group coalitions summed over time, with lagging influence, but which develop interests and capabilities of their own. Skowroneck (1982) and other political scientists recently have devoted substantial attention to the development of administrative capabilities in American governmental institutions.

A biological analogy is useful here. Genetics shape human potential and behavior, but environmental factors also influence behavior. The answer to which shapes behavioral outputs is not simply one or the other; both factors affect human behavior. The interesting questions are: How do they interact? and To what extent is genetics destiny? Similarly, it is reasonable to expect that both interests and institutions shape policy decisions. The key questions are: How do they interact? and How much discretion do institutional actors develop and retain after political coalitions establish them and interest group power changes?

Members of regulatory institutions have varied options when they weigh competing input from interest groups. The can act as a cash register and go with the direction of the prevailing interest group forces. Or, political entrepreneurs may rally support for a cause they think is latent and underrepresented in regulatory proceedings, such as small consumers. Other regulators may become convinced of the importance for the macroeconomy of efficient microeconomic policies, or that promotion of economic development is paramount. The choices regulators make are shaped by the actors to whom they are most accountable, their degree of understanding of complicated issues, which is partly a function of their resources such as staff and budget, and the commissioners' backgrounds and attitudes towards regulation.

Regulatory Structure

The regulatory structure explanation stresses the importance of institutional factors in regulatory decisions. It explains why regulators respond differently to interest group pressures. Regulators might develop different definitions and understandings of the issues depending on those to whom they are directly accountable and on the resources available.

Public utility commissions are diverse in scope and institutional form. Some regulate several other industries, such as insurance, banking, transportation, and cable television, while most regulate only water, gas, electric and telecommunications utilities. Most states have protected regulators from direct electoral accountability to allow them latitude to make unpopular decisions in rate cases, to maintain the financial health of the utilities, and to stand up against judicial review. Typical methods for protecting regulators include separate commission budgets financed by utility assessments rather than legislative authorizations, appointment of regulators by the governor, and long terms in office. Most states rely on utility assessments for commission budgets, many utilize gubernatorial appointments, and all have regulatory appointments of four or more years.

While state public utility commissioners are generally insulated from direct voter and legislative accountability through their appointment by the governor, in eleven states citizens elect commissioners directly, and in two others the legislators elect them. It is still debated whether or not electing commissioners affects policy outcomes. Consumer advocates frequently argue for elected commissioners, believing that they do favor consumer interests. Other analysts favor appointment of commissioners, fearing that elected commissioners will favor consumers' short-run interests and leave the utilities undercapitalized in the future (Navarro, 1985). Initially it was expected that elected commissioners would respond to consumers' (that is, voters') pleas that rates be kept low in the near term, which would be expressed in low residential prices and low rates of returns for regulated utilities. While early research on the election of commissioners suggests an effect on regulatory outcomes in favor of consumers, the inclusion of economic variables in the analyses far outweighs any impact on rates caused by commissioner selection (Pelsoci, 1979; Costello, 1984). The issue is not resolved, as studies that include economic variables have found that electing commissioners does lead to decisions favoring short-run residential consumer interests (Mann and Primeaux, 1983; Navarro, 1985).

The amount and type of other resources available to commissioners may also affect their decisions.[2] Such resources include budget, staff, and data processing capability (Gormley, 1983). The regulatory staff is the most essential resource regulators command. Since divestiture, while commissioners have faced several difficult policy choices in telecommunications, other regulatory areas, including nuclear power and hazardous waste disposal, have demanded their attention as well. With these other demands and the complexities of telecommunications issues, it is no surprise that overloaded commissioners depend greatly on their staffs. Larger staffs should lead to better and more complete analysis: 27 states had staff units solely dedicated to telecommunications issues in 1986. Of course, the composition of the staff may be as important as its size or exclusivity. Traditional utility regulation relies upon accountants, engineers, and lawyers. In the current telecommunications environment, these skills need to be supplemented by those of economists, policy analysts, and statisticians, especially if commissioners seek to change telecommunications policy.

Contemporary utility regulation involves at least three phases; day-to-day staff activities, the formal process of administrative law, and the informal process (Joskow, 1972). Regulatory staffs play an important role in each phase. Many scholars argue that staffs play a stronger role in influencing commissioners than do outside interest groups, such as utility lobbyists and consumer groups (Gormley, 1983; O'Toole and Montjoy, 1984; Meier, 1988). The extent of this role depends on the complexity of the issues and the need for continuing staff involvement (Anderson, 1981). Telecommunications issues are complex and require continual monitoring.

While larger commissions and larger staffs should lead to better analysis, regulatory agency size may affect decision-making in another manner. The decision-makers themselves and their staffs hold a vested interest in continuing regulation of telecommunications to expand their influence, or at least, to keep their jobs (see Niskanen, 1971).[3] It is plausible that larger regulatory staffs could lead to less deregulation in a state. On the federal level, however, regulators and key staff members (who, after all, are most likely to be policy entrepreneurs) often received lucrative employment offers outside of government, based on their experience and industry knowledge developed during the deregulatory process. Bureaucratic inertia did not prevent the abolition of the Civil Aeronautics Board or substantial staff reductions in the Interstate Commerce Commission on the federal level. Furthermore, even in states where telecommunications deregulation has been implemented, staffs have not been cut; much activity remains for staffs to analyze and monitor.

Regulatory Attitudes

The other part of the institutional theory of regulation contends that the attitudes or ideology of commissioners and the legislators that oversee them are the crucial determinants of decisions. Interest group input comes to commissioners from a multitude of sources and regulators need to sort out these arguments. While their accountability structure and resources affect how they process this informational input, regulators' own ideological views and backgrounds shape the emphasis they place on equity, efficiency, and stability of outcomes. While efficiency in prices is an important goal, debates about telephone policy also focus on basic issues of societal access and communications rights that were nurtured for decades under the service-oriented Bell system monopoly.

Several recent attempts to separate the impact of interest group inputs from ideological influences form a so-called Harvard School capture/ideology framework (Leone and Jackson, 1981; Kalt, 1981;

Kalt and Zupan, 1984; Navarro, 1985). The questions of how separable ideology may be from these other influences and how to measure it are difficult to answer (see, for example, Kingdon, 1988), and I shall characterize regulatory attitudes along several different dimensions.

Some regulators see their role in active terms, as political entrepreneurs, while others view regulation as reactive and caretaking (Miles and Bhambri, 1983). Some regulators clearly have further political ambitions and seek higher elected or appointed offices. Others are political patronage job holders, although such appointments are made less often today than in the quiescent past of utility regulation.[4] Regulators perform executive, legislative, and judicial functions, which some refer to as "the trinity of governmental power" (Smith, 1984). They hold a wide scope of power that can be utilized aggressively or minimized.

The regulators' attitudes are likely to be linked to several variables. Party identification is the most elemental political variable. Regulators' party affiliation may influence the emphasis they place on efficiency and different economic interests. Republicans are traditionally more business-oriented than Democrats, who are linked more closely to consumer causes. Cross-state studies of policy outcomes, however, do not confirm systematic differences between Republican and Democratic public utility commissioners (Gormley, 1983). The party identification of individual regulators may be too general a measure to influence specific regulatory decisions.

The occupational background of commissioners is linked to different approaches to regulatory problems at the federal and state levels, particularly by lawyers and economists (Katzman, 1980; Gormley, 1983). Although few states require expertise in any particular field related to regulation, a larger percentage of regulators are lawyers than economists, which may affect the emphasis on procedural solutions versus market solutions.[5]

Other regulatory attitudes may affect decision-making in a manner not captured by party identification or occupational background. One is the regulatory tradition and precedents in a state. Regulators' general perceptions of the tradeoff between utilities' long-term financial health and current consumer rates should be fundamental in their telecommunications decisions. Wall Street analysts use the concept of a regulatory climate to capture these attitudes of regulators. These regulatory climate assessments can and do change when new regulators are appointed.

How much influence governors have on regulatory decisions, through their appointment power, is an important theoretical question. In almost all of the non-election states, governors appoint the chairperson of the commission. Only rarely do state regulatory issues become major issues for state governors—for example, Governor White's 1982 gubernatorial race in Texas and Governor Cuomo's 1986 emphasis on the regulators' handling of the Shoreham nuclear plant in New York. Governors prefer to stay away from the "zero-sum," high-conflict issues that regulators face (Gormley, 1983).

While scholars analyze how legislatures and chief executives influence bureaucrats at the federal level (Arnold, 1979; Moe, 1982, 1985; Weingast and Moran, 1983; Schwartz and McCubbins, 1984), little research has been carried out on the state level. Governors avoid direct intervention in difficult regulatory decisions, and state legislators might be expected to follow the same logic (Gormley, 1983). Yet, we will see in Chapters 7 and 8, that governors and legislators play a major part in state telecommunications decisions.

Scholarly interest in Congressional influence over bureaucracies has led to a theory of "Congressional dominance" that utilizes a principal-agent structure (Mitnick, 1980; Weingast and Moran, 1983; but see Moe, 1985). Placing legislative–bureaucratic interaction into a principal-agent framework, legislators employ bureaucrats, such as regulatory commissioners and their staffs, to implement their policies because this is efficient. Legislators, especially those on the relevant subcommittees, must be able to monitor the performance of their bureaucratic agents to ensure that appropriate policies are implemented. Public utility regulators, however, have traditionally and explicitly been given great latitude to make technical decisions. Thus, although their oversight is important, we should not expect governors and legislators to dominate regulatory choices completely.

State Innovation

Previous research finds that states differ significantly in their propensity to adopt policy innovations in regulation and in other areas. In 1969, Walker aggregated innovations in states across several policy areas and constructed an index for each of the 50 states. Differences in the propensity to adopt innovations may reflect elements of state "political culture" not captured by other interest group or institutional factors related to a particular policy, such as telecommunications regulation (Wright et al., 1987). In the course of testing the other hypotheses related to these theories, I test to see if Walker's Index still has explanatory power in state telecommunications regulation.

THEORETICAL SUMMARY

Any empirical test of the theories presented above must analyze regulatory change as a function of the interaction of interest group and institutional factors. More specifically, interest group inputs and contextual conditions shape the external influences, or demand, while the regulatory structures and commissioners' attitudes determine how these influences are perceived and processed, leading to the supply of policy. When the external influences approach equilibrium on a given issue, the independent role of regulatory institutions becomes important.

More formally, the theory is as follows:

Regulatory Change = f (P1, P2, ... Pi; RS; RA; CT)

When P1 through Pi represent the power of interest
groups 1 through i;
RS is regulatory structure;
RA is regulatory attitudes; and
CT is contextual (economic and technological) conditions.

On a given issue, define S as the ratio of the strength of interest group coalitions such that:

S = Sum of Pi PRO / Sum of Pi CON

When $S = 1$, we have equilibrium among the power of interest group coalitions. When S reaches some value sufficiently greater than 1, the power of the "pro" interest group coalition will be enough to force the regulatory change, regardless of regulatory structure and attitudes. There is a point beyond which government institutions can not act contrary to coalitions of very powerful external forces. Conversely, when S reaches some value sufficiently less than 1, the power of the "con" interest group coalition will be enough to block the regulatory change, regardless of regulatory structure and attitudes. (The sufficient value less than 1 is essentially the inverse of the sufficient value greater than 1, although it may differ due to regulatory inertia; it is often easier to block a change than to achieve one). When S is near 1, regulators have more scope to make choices based on the structure of their accountability to other political actors and based on their own judgments.

This model is essentially a political support model like Peltzman's (1976) that adds institutional influence when external support nears an equilibrium. I shall use it in the quantitative analysis and case studies in Chapters 5–8 to analyze cross-sectional regulatory variance. It also can be used to explain regulatory changes over time. In the days when regulated firms captured regulators, S was well above 1, simply because there were no other important, organized interest groups. It did not much matter who the regulators were at that time, and regulation was of the "demand-pull" variety, favoring the regulated. Organized consumer interests and the political pressure of competitors and large users, often spurred on by technological changes, led to S falling closer to 1, which made deregulation possible (although not inevitable) in some industries and in some jurisdictions where enough of the "supply-push" elements were in place.

In state decisions about whether to change the structure of telecommunications prices, the coalition in favor includes the Bell Operating Companies, representing the traditional capture story, and the large users that otherwise can leave the network. The coalition against price changes includes small consumers, who may be inattentive prior to actual changes except for government-funded advocates, and potential competitors, who are more powerful in telecommunications regulation than normally perceived.

The regulated firms and their competitors actively participate in regulatory processes in all states. In some large states, both large business users and small consumer interests are active and powerful. In some small states, neither group is so important. One coalition vastly overpowers the other in only a very few states. Thus, my general theoretical hypothesis is that interest group influence approaches an equilibrium (S is near 1) in most states and we must analyze institutional variables to explain regulatory decisions.

CONCLUSIONS

The two main theories to be tested are the interest group theory and the institutional theory. The interest group theory incorporates the strength of interest groups that provide input into the regulatory process from several different angles, the cleavages that develop on key issues, and the coalitions that form along these cleavages.

The institutional theory argues that the accountability structure of regulatory institutions constrains the evaluation of interest group inputs and the subsequent decisions. The attitudes of regulators affect their decisions independently of interest group pressure and the structure of the commission. I expect that elements of both explanations are required to explain state telecommunications regulatory choices in the 1980s.

Before testing these theories, I shall provide more background on the essential economic and competitive issues faced by state regulators. In Chapter 3, I shall explain the economics of telecommunications networks and state regulatory options after 1982.

3 Telecommunications Economics and State Regulatory Options

The economics of telecommunications networks follow technological changes over time and help to shape the bounds of the pricing and competition policy options available to federal and state regulators. I have discussed the two different pricing philosophies prevelant in telecommunications regulation since the 1920s, the station-to-station and the board-to-board concepts. Each holds different implications for the incomes of affected interest groups, and, therefore, the debate between them is a political issue.

The debate between the station-to-station and board-to-board philosophies became even more important after divestiture, however, as large users developed competitive options outside of the shared network. As a result, economists have devoted substantial effort to clarifying costs and efficient telecommunications rate structures. The analysis is complicated and a thorough understanding requires some knowledge of contemporary industrial organization theories and techniques. In this chapter I explain the basic economics of telecommunications networks, which have constrained the policy options available to regulators, and summarize actual federal and state pricing trends after 1982.

TELECOMMUNICATIONS ECONOMICS

Telecommunications networks provide a variety of services to different customers using the same facilities, including switches, trunk lines, and access lines connecting users. How different customers should be charged for these services is a matter of public policy and will remain so as long as some providers of the services hold market power and competition cannot be relied upon completely to force prices to their appropriate levels. To explore the public policy options fully, the significant elements of network design and costs must be examined.

Network Design

The local telecommunications exchange consists of a series of access loops, generally copper wire (although increasingly glass or "fiber") running from each subscriber's residence or business to a large central switch. The switches are now increasingly electronic, often capable of digital transmission, and run by computer software. An average switch in the United States connects 10,000 access lines.

The access loops are paired wires that run from switches (an average of about two miles) through underground conduit in large bundles and then in smaller groups to subscriber premises. At the subscriber premises, access loops connect to inside wire, and ultimately, a telephone instrument. On the extreme opposite end of the access loop, at the switch, part of the loop physically attaches to the switch itself.

All of this access equipment is termed non-traffic-sensitive (NTS) because its size and costs do not vary with the amount of calls made.[1] NTS costs represent a major portion, and in some cases a majority, of local telephone costs. Due to substantial economies of scale, NTS loop plant is laid out in advance of actual service need. It would be too expensive to dig up two miles of road every time a new loop is needed. This advanced placement of plant, plus high standards of service developed under the AT&T monopoly, makes for much spare loop capacity at any given point.[2] The fill factor, a ratio of current working loop mileage to total mileage, is about .40 across the United States. In addition, the average working access loop is in use only five minutes during the busiest hour of the day (Cornell and Noll, 1985). Thus, loop plant is extensive, expensive, and only in use a small percentage of the time.

This NTS plant, however large relative to usage needs, provides each subscriber with instant access to the network of telecommunications switches, trunk lines, and ultimately, other subscribers. The central office switches connect calls along trunk lines to other central office switches, to still larger trunk lines for long distance calls. The amount of equipment needed is based on the volume of traffic contributed by all users over a given route. Therefore, the costs of this equipment are traffic-sensitive (TS), shared, and caused by usage.

A question can be raised about the NTS and TS engineering tradeoffs in the network. Specifically, do we need so many loops and do they need to be so long? These tradeoffs have large effects on the costs and thus, the proper price, of access. At the extreme, one could envision a national telephone system with a giant switch in either the geographic or population center of the United States with all lines running to it. Then, NTS costs would be enormous and the marginal switching costs of all calls in the United States would be almost zero. This implies pricing with a huge monthly flat-rate access charge and a miniscule price per call. Clearly this would be a cumbersome, expensive system.

In the other extreme scenario, every few houses or telephone lines would share a microchip, so that shared trunk lines would come earlier in the network, more TS equipment would be shared by customers, and less NTS plant would be dedicated to each subscriber.[3] Monthly flat-rate access costs would be lower than today and usage fees would be higher.

How *should* a network be developed? It should be designed at the lowest *total* cost. Then, the costs of access and usage should be recovered in the most efficient pricing system possible. Is today's network designed that way? No one really knows for sure because most network design decisions were made by a regulated monopoly with different incentives and were probably subject to various regulatory distortions (Cornell and Noll, 1985). Whatever the answer to this question, the costs of the current network and its future additions must be paid for in some manner to be decided by public policy.

Problems in Telephone Pricing

Telephone pricing is so difficult and controversial, in part, because telephone networks provide multiple products using some of the same facilities. Access, local usage, intraLATA toll, intrastate inter-LATA toll, WATS, private line services, PBX, Centrex, and pay telephone services all are provided by the same basic system. Furthermore, as cost differences can define essentially different products, a toll call from New York to Chicago is a different product from a toll call from New York to Little Rock. And, at different times of day, calls from two identical points are actually different services because of peak usage differentials.[4]

Even given a network that is designed efficiently, and well-defined services, telephone pricing is difficult in reality because regulators must deal with two types of costs. The first are embedded costs, which are historical or book costs. The second are marginal or incremental costs, which are forward looking, economic costs. Regulators need to determine the total rate base for utilities to establish a proper rate-of-return, or accounting profit.[5] The rate base is determined by the embedded costs of past investments in the network. These costs match auditable accounting reports of the company.

Economists are more concerned with marginal or incremental costs.[6] Incremental costs are forward-looking and based on best available current technology. They are the costs of the next increment of service to be added.

Incremental costs are difficult to determine precisely. Nevertheless, they are used to set efficient prices as they give consumers the proper signals to compare the value they place on a service with society's (and the telephone company's) cost of providing the service. Furthermore, incremental costs are important in a competitive environment because competitors will price incrementally.[7]

A further complication is the continuation of the historical battle between board-to-board and station-to-station pricing, addressed in the 1931 Supreme Court case of *Smith vs. Illinois Bell.* Many analysts stick with the station-to-station argument that toll prices should reflect some of the costs of access lines as they use these lines to complete calls. Alfred Kahn (1984) and other economists dispute this view by arguing that the demand for access itself causes the costs and toll or local usage does not increase these costs. Some advocates of the station-to-station view are not convinced.

Several prominent economists have clarified the efficient prices of the many services provided by the telephone network.[8] Research on two-part tariffs, usage pricing, peak load pricing, network externalities, demand elasticities, and cost function subadditivity supports the following conclusions.

Efficient Prices

At a first cut, efficient prices require a flat rate for network access and incremental cost-based prices for all local and toll usage, matching the board-to-board view of pricing. Access to the switched network is a separate service from usage as access allows incoming calls to be received without any outgoing usage, and access lines are related to individual subscribers, while usage equipment is shared.

Externalities are positive or negative impacts on third parties from transactions in which they are not involved. There are no incentives to consider these impacts in private pricing arrangements and they can therefore justify public policy intervention. The classic negative externality is environmental pollution. Telecommunications networks exhibit elements of positive externalities.

There are two externalities in telephone pricing. The first, the call externality, exists because telephone companies charge the initiator of a call only, rather than both parties to a call. Getting a call is a positive externality for the recipient (unless he or she does not want that call, in which case it is a negative externality). This externality is not generally considered a public policy concern because private parties can handle it themselves easily by sharing initiation of calls in a manner they decide is equitable.

The second externality is the network access externality. The more subscribers on the network, the more valuable it is to all of its subscribers. Since each new subscriber adds to the value all existing subscribers receive from the network, access should be priced somewhat less than its individual marginal cost to account for this incremental value or consumer surplus added to these other subscribers. There is no reason to believe, however, that each existing subscriber puts the same dollar value on the addition of a particular new subscriber. Nevertheless, the policy result is that access should be priced at something less than its cost. The revenue shortfall can be made up by increased usage rates.

Local measured service (LMS) should be charged rather than flat-rate local service with unlimited free calling, if the reduced usage at peak times allows a smaller common switching and trunking network whose cost savings exceed the costs of measurement and billing of local calls. Most empirical studies of LMS have shown this to be true (Crew and Dansby, 1983; Bell Communications Research 1984; although Johnson and Park, 1986 suggest otherwise, depending on local characteristics).

There are many costs in the telephone network that are common to local and toll services. Switches, for example, are used for both local and toll calls.[9] Other common costs include the salaries and overhead for executive officers of a company providing several services. These costs are often allocated to services based on usage criteria, which are arbitrary from an economic standpoint. The proper economic methodology for recovery of these costs is by Ramsey pricing.

Marginal cost pricing will not recover all of these common costs when marginal costs are below average costs. Telephone firms need to recover the fixed costs of equipment, such as switches. Thus, Ramsey pricing marks up prices above cost for those services with the most inelastic demand (Ramsey 1927; Baumol and Bradford, 1970), to keep the overall reduction in consumer surplus at a minimum. Since the demand for access is far more inelastic than the demand for usage, access prices are marked up first and most under Ramsey pricing. Some economists suggest that in practice, the Ramsey price adjustment to cover common telephone costs would roughly offset the downward adjustment in access prices to account for the network externalities (Ordover and Willig, 1983; Perl, 1985).

There are several other possible refinements to cost-based telephone pricing. One is putting a price on uncompleted calls. About one-third of all calls encounter busy signals or no answer. Although we do not charge for these calls, at peak time they place a cost on the network by using scarce switching and trunking equipment. Despite its theoretical accuracy, no regulator has seriously suggested putting a price on uncompleted calls.

Thus, most economists suggest that efficient prices require reductions in current long distance rates, elimination of free, unlimited local calling, and initiation of an explicit subscriber access line charge that is independent of local or long distance usage. The growth of competition in long distance will tend to force prices in this direction.

Opposing Views

Some economists and other analysts find the above policy prescriptions flawed. The most prominent dissent comes from those holding the station-to-station view of pricing. Since local and toll calls require the presence of access lines, the dissenting argument is that the prices of these calls should contribute to recovering access costs. They also argue that the "stand alone" cost of a network providing only access and local usage would be less than the costs of the current network that allows long distance calls to be made as well. Most proponents of this view will agree that the actual distribution of access costs to these other services is arbitrary, but they promote minutes of peak usage as a reasonable distributional criterion.

A subset of this view is that the demand for access is derived from the demand for usage and should be considered in the price structure (Copeland and Severn, 1985). In this view, no one demands access for its own sake, but for the ability to use the switched network. Advocates of this view also argue that toll calls should contribute to the recovery of NTS costs.

Another dissent is that access and usage are not really so clearly separable on a NTS and TS basis (Wilson, 1983). Wilson argues that shared switching could come earlier in the network, and the efficiency of sharing would depend on the amount of usage. This is clearly true with PBXs, for example, where office building or apartment tenants can reduce the number of incoming access lines by sharing them and having the "smart" switch allocate access to usage trunk lines. The amount of access lines necessary for service would depend on the peak calling usage characteristics of the tenants. Thus, access lines are non-traffic-sensitive only when there is little concern about call blockage due to limited usage, as in the case of a residence with one line. With shared usage, however, the amount of access plant necessary becomes based on usage criteria, and the neat NTS/TS separation breaks down.[10]

There are additional, practical problems with the prevailing view of efficient telephone prices described in the previous section. Even proponents of efficient pricing admit that there are many difficulties in determining costs with precision (Kahn, 1984). Furthermore, the information currently available to decision-makers is lacking, and many practical measures of the cross-subsidy from usage to access may be overstated (Cornell and Noll, 1985). In addition, a Rand study has challenged the established view of economists that local measured service is efficient, as digital technology makes switching costs miniscule (Johnson and Park, 1986).

Good Public Policy

Not all of these opposing views have merit. The station-to-station view is flawed because benefits are confused with costs (Kahn, 1984). Toll calls do benefit from the presence of access lines, but if they do not cause an increase in access costs, then they should not contribute to access cost recovery.[11] Telephone instruments are necessary on both ends for the completion of any call, but we do not expect toll prices to contribute to the cost of telephone instruments.

The argument that access is not a priceable service on its own is without merit. Subscribers desire access to receive incoming calls even if they *never* make any outgoing toll or local calls. Access has a specific cost associated with it regardless of whether or not the demand for access is derived. To extend the previous analogy, the demand for telephone instruments is derived from telephone usage but we do not therefore expect usage prices to contribute to the cost of telephone instruments.

Much of the confusion about efficient pricing is caused by a lack of understanding of network externalities. Those who dissent understand that the network would be less valuable to everyone with fewer subscribers and then jump to the conclusion that access must be priced far below its cost to maximize subscribership. That access should be priced somewhat below its cost to account for the network externality is true, but the amount is measurable (Ordover and Willig, 1983), and economists estimate it to be between $1.50 and $4.00 per month (Danner, 1986; Perl, 1985). Some economists argue that Ramsey pricing to recover common costs may counteract some of this reduction in access prices caused by the network externality.[12]

The objections of John Wilson (1983) are much more difficult to refute. It does seem clear that NTS and TS tradeoffs can be made in designing parts of a network. To some extent, however, as Kahn (1984) notes, all subscribers must live with society's choices to minimize total network costs. Furthermore, as with all the other objections, in practice there is an important additional force driving pricing decisions toward efficiency. If toll call prices are not reduced closer to cost, concentrated large users hold the potential to bypass the network. A very small number of such users account for a very large percentage of toll revenues in most states. In New York, for example, 0.3 percent of business customers represent 33 percent of toll usage. With existing technologies, it is relatively easy for these firms to become self-providers of telecommunications services for their own internal traffic. Recovery of NTS costs through usage provides a large incentive to bypass.[13]

While analysts agree that uneconomic bypass caused by pricing not based on costs would drive up costs for all users, they debate intensely the actual potential for bypass. Economists argue that toll calls priced 100–200 percent above costs provided a tremendous incentive to bypass. Others argue that many large firms have already bypassed as much as they wish to by using on-site PBXs for internal local calling and private lines provided by the telephone company for internal long distance point-to-point communications. Studies after divestiture, however, have found that many firms are considering further bypass (Kraemer, 1985).

Opponents of efficient prices argue that the likelihood of large-scale bypass is low because many firms do not want to get into the tele-communications business, they do not want the management problems, and they will gladly pay more to be served by the local telephone company. This argument is flawed, however, because several new consulting firms, staffed with ex-telephone company engineers, can provide telecommunications management functions for large users.

STATE REGULATORY OPTIONS

After divestiture, state regulators have had several options to deal with pricing and competitive issues given these network economics. They could have embraced the suggestions of economists to increase end-user access prices while dropping toll rates and allowing competition. Alternatively, regulators could have maintained existing cross-subsidies and blocked new competitive entrants. Or, they could have mixed elements of these different policies.

Cost-based usage prices, accompanied by flat end-user access charges, should be implemented to avoid large-scale bypass of the network. If regulators change rates gradually, but not too slowly, they can avoid large-scale uneconomic bypass and then monitor the changes in telecommunications markets as the prices are adjusted. For those users with high access elasticity who will disconnect from the network if access prices grow substantially, targeted subsidies are appropriate, through "lifeline" programs. This is a relatively small group, roughly corresponding to welfare recipients, as shown in Table 3.1.

It may also be necessary to subsidize rural customers to make gradual the large increases in their cost-based access prices. For the bulk of residential consumers, however, the subsidy to access has been large and perhaps unnecessary to achieve universal service over the past fifteen years. As Roger Noll (1986) notes, "It is a transfer of too much from too few to too many in too inefficient a manner" (p. 192).

The options for state telephone regulators after divestiture can be arrayed along a continuum. At one extreme is the choice to move

Table 3.1

Telephone Penetration and Household Income

HH INCOME	PERCENTAGE OF HHs WITH TELEPHONE
under $5,000	71.1
$5,000-7,499	82.7
$7,500-9,999	87.6
$10,000-12,499	89.5
$12,500-14,999	91.3
$15,000-17,499	92.9
$17,500-19,999	94.6
$20,000+	96.3

Data from U.S. Census Bureau, 1986

rapidly to efficient prices and let the distributional consequences occur as they may. On the opposite extreme is a policy of retaining the old methods of cost allocation. The first policy extreme implies opening markets to competition rapidly. The latter implies not allowing competitive entry for as long as possible to maintain the cross-subsidies inherent in the old rate structure. In between these two extremes are a large number of policy combinations or different timing schedules.

ACTUAL POLICY AFTER 1982

State policy choices are not made in a vacuum. They have been and continue to be heavily influenced by federal policy decisions. The Federal Communications Commission's decisions from 1982 through 1989 followed largely the board-to-board pricing perspective, although Congressional fears of consumer rebellion were reflected in the continued use of limited cross-subsidies. State decisions, while varied, generally supported the station-to-station perspective and attempted to raise revenues from sources other than local residential rates.

Federal Regulatory Actions

After divestiture, the FCC considered pure and mixed strategies to shift access costs from usage to network subscribers and adopted a mixed strategy that initiated business and residential end-user charges. The FCC established business charges of $6.00 per month for multiline users in 1984. Congress grew concerned about the FCC's schedule for residential customer access line charges (CALCs), which were slated to start at $2.00 per month in 1984, rising annually to a $7.00 level in 1989. Congress pressured the FCC into delaying the CALC until June 1985, and lowering it to $1.00 in 1985 and $2.00 in 1986.[14] A subsequent compromise led to further increases, with a ceiling of $3.50 set for 1989.

The FCC made several important decisions on depreciation issues, interstate revenue pooling arrangements, lifeline programs, and other issues with interstate dimensions. They initiated a lifeline program that more than half the states had joined by 1989, which reduced eligible residential rates by twice the amount of the federal CALC, and a program to subsidize installation rates for eligible consumers.

The FCC generally expanded its regulatory jurisdiction whenever areas of uncertainty developed (Noam, 1983; Maher, 1985). As Kenneth Robinson, of the National Telecommunications and Information Administration, notes: "It has certainly been the case at the federal level for 20 years that state regulators have been viewed as poor relations.... Federal agencies have viewed them with suspicion and guarded distrust." (Teske, 1987, p. 6). Courts generally rejected state efforts to avoid implementation of the spirit of FCC decisions. The 1986 *Louisiana PSC vs. FCC* depreciation case halted this trend and affirmed two-tiered regulation by upholding state regulatory jurisdiction on issues with largely intrastate implications.

State Regulatory Decisions

While state decisions varied from 1982 through 1986, they can be summarized. State regulators approved $10.5 billion in rate hikes from 1982 to 1986, out of $70 billion in annual BOC revenues.[15] The highwater point of these increases was 1984 in which $3.9 billion in rate hikes were approved, representing 53 percent of telephone company requests. In 1982, $2.9 billion were approved (55 percent of requests), $2.4 billion in 1983 (40 percent), and $1.3 billion in 1985 (45 percent). Thus, the telephone companies sought substantial rate relief in the five years after the Consent Decree and state regulators granted about half of the requests.

Much of this increase in rates did not fall on local service. "State Commissions have generally chosen to increase rates for special business services, intrastate toll and enhanced services before increasing rates for basic residential local exchange services" (*National Association of Regulatory Utility Commissioners Bulletin*, 1986, p. 15). In Table 3.2, consumer price index (CPI) figures show annual increases

Table 3.2

Consumer Price Index Changes

	OVERALL	TELEPHONE RATES
1981	8.9%	11.8%
1982	3.9%	7.3%
1983	3.8%	3.6%
1984	4.0%	9.2%
1985	3.8%	4.7%
1986	1.1%	2.7%
1987	4.4%	-1.3%
1988	4.4%	1.3%

Data from U.S. Bureau of Labor Statistics.

for total telephone service for urban consumers. Telephone rates increased faster than general inflation from 1981 through 1986; in 1987 total telephone rates decreased. In contrast, the increases in telephone prices were consistently far below the general inflation rate in 1978–80, rising 1 percent, 1 percent, and 4.5 percent, respectively.

The U.S. Department of Commerce argues that the increases in telephone costs after the divestiture are not significantly different from those prior to divestiture (National Telecommunications and Information Administration, 1985). However, as Table 3.3 shows, *local* telephone rates (including equipment, installation, enhanced services

Table 3.3

CPI Indices of Telephone Costs

	LOCAL RATES	INTRASTATE TOLL	INTERSTATE TOLL
1981	12.6%	6.1%	14.6%
1982	10.8%	4.1%	2.6%
1983	3.2%	7.4%	1.4%
1984	17.1%	3.7%	-4.3%
1985	8.9%	0.5%	-3.8%
1986	7.1%	0.4%	-9.5%
1987	5.2%	-2.7%	-12.6%
1988	4.5%	-4.2%	-4.2%

Data from U.S. Bureau of Labor Statistics.

Table 3.4

Telephone Rate Increase Requests

	DOLLARS (MILL.)	NUMBER OF CASES
1980	1,493	42
1981	2,912	67
1982	2,621	59
1983	3,043	80
1984	2,295	44
1985	1,018	43
1986	250	23

Data from Regulatory Research Associates.

and taxes) increased substantially above inflation after 1982, while toll rates increased less than the CPI or even decreased. Interstate toll prices increased less (and, in fact, decreased after 1983) than intrastate toll rates after 1982 because the FCC was more aggressive in changing rate structures than were state regulators.

Several groups attempt to quantify the impact of these increases on the average residential consumer. The Consumer Federation of America calculates that residential rates rose an average of 35 percent for flat-rate service and 52 percent for measured service from 1984 to 1986. Their figures show that the average residential flat rate grew from $10.55 to $14.29 per month, while the cheapest average message rate grew from $5.15 to $7.81 per month. The FCC estimates that the national average flat rate local bill increased from $11.51 in 1984 to $14.14 in 1986, a 23 percent increase. Whichever figures are more accurate, 23–52 percent represent large percentage changes, but $2.00–3.00 per month are not large absolute increases.

Thus, state regulators approved substantial rate increases after the 1982 Consent Decree. As Table 3.4 shows, the Consent Decree for divestiture increased the pace of filings, but the pace slowed in 1985 and dropped substantially in 1986. Apart from divestiture, telephone companies also increased their requests in the early 1980s to make up for inadequate rate increases that regulators kept below the rate of inflation in the late 1970s and because of high interest rates. By 1986, these macroeconomic conditions had improved and the 1986 federal Tax Reform Act reduced the tax liability of most telephone firms.

CONCLUSIONS

State regulators have faced several important policy choices after the divestiture of the local operating companies from AT&T. Most economists argue that regulators should reduce toll rates and increase local access charges, to increase efficiency and to avoid network bypass by large toll users.

Actual state choices have followed a general pattern. Sharon Nelson, Washington state regulator and President of the National Association of Regulatory Utility Commissioners, divides the post-divestiture period into three phases of state regulation. The first, from 1984 through 1986, the period analyzed most closely in this book, she calls the "reaction" period. The second, from 1987 through 1989, is the "retrenchment" period, when rapid rate increases were halted, in part because of the federal Tax Reform Act. The third phase Nelson expects is a "restructuring" period in the 1990s.

While state regulators did raise local rates after 1984, they did not increase them so much as economists suggest, nor did they cut intrastate toll rates so much as federal regulators cut interstate rates. In the 1990s, consumers are paying more for local service, but states vary greatly in the sizes of the increase they have imposed upon consumers. The next step is to understand how these proposed and actual price changes affect different interest groups and how these groups have organized to fight for favorable pricing and competition policies.

4

Interest Group
Formation

American citizens and the officials they elect care greatly about the private market's distribution of benefits and costs. Changes in the organization and pricing of telecommunications services created by the divestiture of AT&T and subsequent Federal Communications Commission decisions drastically altered the nature of market activity for telecommunications services and hence altered the distribution of income. The citizens who believe they will suffer losses from the pricing of telecommunications services at marginal costs are likely to use political activity to resist the negative distributional implications of telecommunications reorganization. In this chapter I investigate whether the commonly believed distributional consequences of marginal cost telecommunications pricing are accurate. Is it true that moderate and low-income residential and small business customers lose while affluent residential and large business customers gain? Does the organization and activity of interests in this policy area reflect the actual distribution of costs and benefits?

Policymakers are concerned about who will be affected by deregulation and the subsequent repricing of telecommunications services. Incidence may not completely determine policy formulation but it certainly is an important factor for the politics of deregulation in every state. The analysis of the incidence of changing telephone rate structures in this chapter focuses on three types of costs and benefits —general, group, and geographic.[1] The costs and benefits of each type are assessed as incentives for interest group formation and participation in the regulatory process. The objective is to clarify the incidence of winners and losers in the short run and long run from telecommunication deregulation to see how economic incidence affects political activity. The analysis compares evidence from other researchers and utilizes original data for the group incidence portion, from the Bureau of Labor Statistics 1984 Consumer Expenditure Survey, comparing economically efficient prices with those extant immediately after the AT&T divestiture.

GENERAL BENEFITS AND COSTS

Two types of general benefits are associated with telecommunications deregulation. First, moving towards prices based on marginal costs reduces the "deadweight loss" from inefficient telecommunications usage prices. This increase in consumers' surplus can be distributed in many ways. Second, deregulation and the ensuing changes in pricing prevent some uneconomic bypass by large users.

The AT&T divestiture also caused nontangible general costs, including the loss of security, convenience and other values that represent important changes from the "Ma Bell" monopoly era.

Price-Cost Comparison

I have already developed the economic arguments for reducing toll rates and increasing end-user access charges. A rigorous analysis of the incidence of changing prices requires a quantification of the trade-off. What flat-rate subscriber access charge is required to balance a given percentage decrease in toll rates? Dr. Lewis Perl suggests that an $11.00 end-user charge was needed, on average, in 1984 to bring prices up to incremental costs, with approximately half of the increase allocated to reducing interstate toll rates and half to intrastate toll rates. Other evidence, from various state studies, suggests that $11.00 was a conservative figure.[2]

The average percentage decrease in toll rates can be determined directly, from data on the number of telephone lines and toll revenues. With about 90 million access lines in the United States before divestiture, a $1.00 monthly flat end-user charge would raise about $1 billion per year. This revenue could have been used to cut intrastate message toll service (MTS) by about 9 percent, to cut interstate message toll rates by 6 percent, or to cut both by about 4 percent.[3]

The estimates vary by region of the country, depending on previous rate structure. For example, NYNEX could have cut intrastate toll (MTS) rates 13.6 percent per $1.00 end-user charge, while Pacific Telesis could only have cut intrastate MTS rates by 6 percent, partly because Pacific Telesis had a higher base figure of intrastate toll revenue for calls within California. On a national basis, a good estimate is that both average intrastate toll rates (in which I am most interested here) and interstate toll rates would drop 20 percent in exchange for a $5.00 monthly increase in end-user charges (or 4 percent per $1.00 end-user charge). This estimate is essential in determining which consumers will gain and lose from the first-order effects of repricing. I will discuss the impact of a different change in toll rates as a result of a $1.00 subscriber charge to determine how sensitive the incidence results are to this estimate.

Benefits

More efficient telecommunications prices will benefit the United States economy because consumers will make additional calls that they value more than the costs caused by such calls. Efficient prices generate more telecommunications usage and an aggregate annual increase in consumer surplus estimated to be between $5-$10 billion (Perl, 1985; Wenders, 1987). The deadweight loss from inefficient pricing represents between 7 percent and 14 percent of the $70 billion in revenues generated by the local telephone operating companies; at the lower figure it represents $77.00 per household per year (Perl, 1985).[4] Efficient prices may also lead to other second-order benefits in addition to stimulated usage. These include a pass-through of business toll rate savings to consumers, more consumer choices, and, possibly, enhanced innovation by competitors over time.

While the economic efficiency arguments are "carrots" that seduced regulators towards changing price structures, the bypass possibilities are "sticks" that tend to force action. The estimates of the likely gains (or, more accurately, prevented losses) from repricing to avoid uneconomic bypass are more problematic than the efficiency gains noted above. Concentrated large users would have taken traffic off the network to avoid paying toll prices set above costs, despite the fact that their bypass costs may have been above the actual incremental costs on the shared network. With the loss of this revenue to bypass, ratepayers remaining on the network would have faced higher rates to support the network facilities, as the regulated local telephone operating companies are allowed to recover their sunk investment costs.

One study attempts to quantify these prevented losses. The Bell Communications Research model estimated net losses per month of $5.85 per line in 1984 if prices were not adjusted. The Bell Core model estimates a $10.20 loss per line per month if prices were not changed and a $4.55 loss to bypass even if prices were changed. The latter figure represents a recognition that some bypass would occur for real economic, technological, or privacy reasons rather than because of the cross-subsidy. The Federal Communications Commission prepared a model that is not directly comparable but which also suggests gains from repricing and preventing bypass. These models have received much criticism (see General Accounting Office Report, 1986). Nevertheless, they illustrate the point that efficiency losses could be prevented by repricing, which must be figured into an analysis of general costs and benefits.

Several state-level bypass studies prepared after divestiture determined that much bypass had already occured in the form of private line connections, and that the potential existed for more bypass (Kraemer, 1985). Oregon, for example, had 59 private microwave systems by 1985, even though few corporate headquarters are located there.

Costs

Consumers have experienced significant noneconomic costs from the deregulation of telecommunications service. By definition, these costs are not easily measurable in dollar terms, but include both confusion and lost time caused by an increase in service problems in the transition after divestiture, and the psychological costs to consumers of facing many new decisions about buying and leasing equipment, maintenance uncertainty, and difficulties of dealing with several bills and suppliers. Regulators realize that these costs are important. Edward Burke, former chair of the Rhode Island public utility commission, notes: "We get the most flak from consumers about the quality of service" (Teske, 1987, p. 6).

Something about the new telecommunications environment must have been troubling to consumers because survey data suggest that a majority do not favor the AT&T breakup and consider it a mistake. Only 25 percent of respondents to both a 1986 Associated Press-General Media poll and a 1985 Louis Harris poll thought that the AT&T divestiture was a good idea.[5]

While survey data can be transient, they help clarify whether residential consumers understood the changes in telecommunications markets and whether they were reacting rationally in economic and political choices to take full advantage of the new situation. The negative response to divestiture and deregulation may have been based on the belief, held by 60 percent of the Associated Press respondents, that the costs of local service had increased (which is true), and on the claim by 20 percent that they considered cancelling telephone service (although national telephone penetration statistics show no significant decrease from 1981 through 1989). Furthermore, a December 1988 Washington Post poll found that more respondents still thought divestiture was a bad idea than the number that thought it was a good idea five years after the event.

Evidence from two states suggests that consumers have not fully understood the telephone service choices open to them, which can be considered a general transition cost; without information, consumers can not make optimal choices. In Maine, New England Telephone has waged a political battle over implementing local measured service. In a binding survey of 85,000 residential consumers, performed by New England Telephone at the order of the Maine public utility commission, 81 percent chose measured service options rather than flat-rate service.[6] When consumers consider their alternatives rationally, they prefer the measured service options, but most consumer groups have opposed the imposition of local measured service, reacting against paying for that which was previously perceived to be free.[7]

The Pennsylvania public utility commission surveyed residential consumers in 1986 about their awareness of telecommunications issues. Consumers generally were unaware of local calling options that could have saved them money: Only 4 percent could identify the local calling options, 15 percent knew about them but could not recall more than one, and 67 percent were unfamiliar with the choices.[8] Clearly consumers have been confused about some of the positive options that resulted from divestiture.

Thus, changes in telecommunications pricing can stimulate additional usage and consumer surplus, and help avoid costly uneconomic bypass, but they also cause confusion for and subsequent opposition from many consumers.

GROUP BENEFITS AND COSTS

Several important groups experience costs and benefits differently from changing rate structures. These groups include large businesses that use telecommunications services intensively, small businesses, and residential consumers. I disaggregate residential consumers by income groups to understand the variable impact of changing prices. The typical assumption that low-income and elderly groups are major losers from efficient pricing policies is not fully accurate. The removal of cross-subsidies results in a far more complicated short-run gain and loss scenario, which helps explain the fragmentation of political coalitions in some states.

Large Users

Virtually all analysts of the changing telecommunications industry environment agree that large businesses benefit most from higher end-user charges and lower toll rates. Indeed, as I argued in Chapter 1, these firms provided a major pull in the direction of divestiture and telecommunications deregulation. Large users subsidized smaller users for many years but have developed new options outside of the shared network facilities. The geographic concentration of business locations with heavy telecommunications traffic allows cost-effective, private connections with microwave, fiber optic, or satellite transmission facilities. Nationally, 1 percent of business locations generate between 45–53 percent of all business telephone traffic (General Accounting Office Report, 1986). White-collar, service industries such as financial firms are the major users of telecommunications services. The most intensive user occupation is stockbrokers, followed by other financial service workers, with transportation, public utility, business service and wholesale trade workers also above average in usage (Coopers and Lybrand, 1987).

Thus, large businesses hold substantial stakes in telephone pricing issues, exhibit elastic demand because they have other options in addition to the shared network, and control many jobs and much economic development in any given state, a potent combination of economic incentives and political levers.

Small Businesses

The impact of repricing on small businesses is less clear. The best evidence comes from a 1984 Bell Communications Research survey of small businesses (although, as with their bypass study, they are not a disinterested party). The study analyzes the impact of a $4.00 subscriber line charge ($6.00 for multiline customers) and a resulting 30 percent drop in interstate toll rates for a sample of 9,085 firms with a range of 1–499 employees.

Interstate toll represents about 45 percent of telephone bills for these firms, on average, and the price shifts lead to an overall 10 percent reduction in average telephone bills. The impacts vary, however, by size and type of business. Only 46 percent of firms with fewer than 10 employees gain, while 62 percent of those with more than 10 employees gain from the first-order effects. For the 54 percent of firms with fewer than 10 employees that lose from repricing, an average of 40 percent of the loss is offset by the toll reductions.

For the smallest of the small businesses, single-line business customers, 56 percent of the firms face an average loss of $2.64 per month from this repricing, and the other 44 percent gain. The average $2.64 loss per month represents a 7.3 percent increase in their average monthly telephone bill. Since telephone expenses are less than 1 percent of sales for all of the sampled firms with fewer than 100 employees, this represents a miniscule (.07 percent at most) increase in the cost of doing business for these firms, which are the hardest hit.

While this study focuses only on *interstate* toll usage, the incidence of price changes on small businesses is likely to be more positive for *intrastate* toll services. Small businesses probably spend proportionately more than larger national and international firms on intrastate toll than on interstate toll because their clientele and distributors are more likely to be located nearby. A parallel analysis should yield an even more positive picture for repricing service within a given state. Thus, small businesses as a group do not have strong incentives either to oppose or favor the restructuring of toll and local prices.

Residential Consumers

Most analysts expect residential consumers as a group to be the largest losers from changing telephone prices, particularly as they have been beneficiaries of several cross-subsidies for decades. The incidence within this category, however, is quite varied. As with the other groups, residential distributional issues depend on the relationship of toll usage to income.

Most superficial analyses predict that changing telephone prices has significant regressive impacts. Many consumer advocates believe that low-income households might be driven from the network or harmed substantially by the increase in access charges and will not gain from toll reductions because they do not make toll calls. Many commentators also believe that the elderly will lose because they make fewer toll calls than other groups and are perceived to be poorer, although statistics do not confirm the latter assumption. Some residences make very few toll calls and face losses from repricing, with an upper-bound limit on the loss of the amount of the end-user charge. Analysts do not know exactly how toll usage relates to income.[9] My analysis uses the 1984 U.S Bureau of Labor Statistics (BLS) Consumer Expenditure Survey to determine how changes in the price structure would affect consumers generally and those in different income groups.[10]

Consumer Expenditure Survey Analysis

While lower-income consumers on average face losses from the first-order impacts of a decision to change prices, many lower-income households would gain and many higher-income households would lose. The variation within income groups is greater than that across groups. Furthermore, this analysis considers only the first-order impacts of price changes and ignores the gain in consumer surplus that would come from the increase in usage under lower toll rates, and the passing-through of lower toll rates from large businesses to consumers in the price of their goods and services.

According to BLS figures, average monthly telephone expenditures for urban residences were $38.00 in 1984. The estimated breakdown by the BLS of the average telephone bill for these consumers included about $19.00 for local service (including access, local usage and other charges, such as touch-tone, call forwarding, etc.), $12.00 for *interstate* toll calls, and $7.00 for *intrastate* toll calls. This matches very closely with 1983 AT&T figures (the last year from which such aggregate figures are publicly available) that show an average residential bill of about $19.00 for local service, $12.00 for interstate toll, and $8.00 for intrastate toll. Both sets of data correspond on an average residential consumer expenditure of $19.00–20.00 per month for toll calls in 1983–1984.[11]

Earlier, I cited Perl's (1985) argument that an $11.00 end-user charge would eliminate most of the cross-subsidy from usage to access (although this was estimated and an average, hiding substantial variation by state and density regions within states). Since about half of this cross-subsidy has been implemented on the national interstate level (the FCC's 1989 customer access line charge was $3.50 per month to reduce this cross-subsidy), I will consider the impacts of a $5.00 intrastate end-user charge in exchange for a 20 percent drop in both intrastate and interstate toll rates. I will also consider the impacts of a 45 percent cut in intrastate toll rates only, in exchange for the $5.00 end-user charge (although the assumptions needed for using the BLS data become more heroic).

The average (mean) residential telephone consumer with $20.00 per month in total (interstate and intrastate) toll calls would see a drop of $4.00 per month in the toll bill in exchange for the $5.00 monthly charge. Thus, the average residential consumer faces losses of $1.00 per month under this repricing structure. If the rate cuts are applied to intrastate toll rates only, the average residential consumer, with an $8.00 monthly intrastate toll bill, would face a $1.40 per month loss from repricing.[12]

If the average residential user faces losses of about $1.00 per month from efficient price changes, what is all the political fuss about? Just as toll-calling patterns are skewed for businesses, this pattern appears, although not so extremely, for residential consumers. About 10 percent of residential users made 50 percent of all residential interstate toll calls in 1982, compared to 1 percent of the largest businesses making nearly half of all business toll calls (Wenders, 1987). To get a more meaningful estimate of the political relevance of price changes, we must look at the distribution of usage and, particularly, at the *median* residential consumer rather than the average one.

The 1983 AT&T data show that the median residential consumer spent $9.00 per month for interstate and intrastate toll calls, substantially less than the $20.00 average. With the above calculation for repricing, such a consumer would lose $3.20 per month, with a $5.00 end-user charge only partially balanced by a 20 percent, or $1.80, decline in the total monthly toll bill.

The 1984 BLS data show that the median residential consumer spent $30.00 per month for the total telephone bill, $8.00 less than the average consumer's total bill. What does this suggest for the median toll expenditure? Assuming, conservatively, that the median consumer spent as much as the average consumer on options applied to the local bill, such as touch-tone, the median toll bill would be $11.00 per month.[13] With a 20 percent cut in both intrastate and interstate toll rates, this median user faces first-order losses of $2.80 per month from the imposition of a $5.00 end-user charge. Assuming that the ratio of intrastate to interstate toll calls is about the same for the median residential consumer as for the average consumer, the $5.00 end-user charge applied only to *intrastate* rates leaves the median consumer $3.00 worse off per month.[14]

How does toll usage vary around the median? Table 4.1 shows the distribution of toll expenditures, assuming an average expenditure on the local bill for all consumers.

Table 4.1

Distribution of Toll Expenditures by Residences

PERCENTAGE OF HOUSEHOLDS BELOW	MONTHLY TOLL EXPENDITURES ($)
99%	150
95%	80
90%	55
75%	28
50%	11
25%	3
10%	1
5%	0
0%	0

Data from 1984 *BLS Consumer Expenditure Survey.*

Table 4.1 shows that 25 percent of all residential consumers made more than $28.00 worth of toll calls in an average 1984 month, 25 percent made between $11.00 and $28.00, another 25 percent made between $3.00 and $11.00 per month, and another 25 percent made $3.00 or less. Consumers in the highest quartile of toll usage are clear winners from the first-order impacts of repricing, by at least $.60 per month. Consumers in the next quartile face losses of as much as $2.80 per month or gains up to $.60 per month. Consumers in the third quartile face losses from $2.80 up to $4.40 per month, while those in the final group face losses from $4.40 to $5.00 per month.

How does this distribution relate to income? The income data in the BLS Survey are problematic. "The lowest income category contains a large number of households with large self-employment losses and people whose income is normally higher for other reasons."[15] Thus, the lowest income quintile reported an average income of only $91.00 in 1984 but reported expenditures of $3,600, suggesting that these are not fully reliable income figures. Furthermore, I am not able to control for other relevant demographic data that affect telephone usage, such as household size, age of head of household, race, and mobility (Brandon, 1981), so a simple regression of income on toll calling may show bias from omitted variables. Nevertheless, since these are the only available data, I will use them in a suggestive analysis.

Toll expenditures are positively related to income and the relationship is highly significant (99.9 percent), with an adjusted R-squared value of 0.06. The beta value is 0.00453, meaning that a $1,000 rise in income, on average, results in a $4.53 increase in annual toll expenditure, and a $10,000 rise in income, on average, results in an $45.30 annual increase in toll expenditure, or nearly $4.00 per month. Such a $4.00 per month increase in toll usage per $10,000 income rise is a significant but not huge difference, compared to the likely extent of price changes necessary to achieve efficiency. On average in 1984, the wealthiest quintile of households spent about twice as much on toll calls as did the poorest quintile.[16]

Despite this positive relationship of income and toll expenditure, income alone is not a strong predictor of toll expenditure. Only 6 percent of the variance in toll expenditure is explained by income differences. These results may show specification bias because of the omission of other relevant variables. Other studies show a significant, positive relationship of income to toll calling, but also with a great deal of variance from unmeasured causes.

How do these results compare to other studies? Toll expenditure data from California in 1983 show that the average household under $10,000 annual income spent $14.00 per month while those with $50,000 and above spent $29.00 per month on toll calls.[17] California data for intrastate toll expenditures only show the distribution across income classes. The average household under $11,000 income, for example, spent $6.60 monthly on toll calls, while the average $50,000+ household spent $11.00 per month, near the 2:1 relationship for all toll calls.[18] The standard deviation was about $10.00 for low-income families and $15.00 for high-income families, and was higher for *all* income categories than the maximum $4.40 difference in mean across all income groups. So, for example, while 43 percent of customers with incomes less than $11,000 in California made less than $3.00 in intrastate toll calls, 29 percent in the middle-income category and 32 percent in the highest income category also made less than $3.00 in intrastate toll calls. These households are clear losers from repricing.

Thus, national data show that, while the average residential household would lose about $1.00 per month from intrastate and interstate price changes, the median household faces losses in the range of $3.00 per month. Toll usage is related to income, but the relationship does not explain a large amount of the variance in toll expenditure, and a substantial minority of residential consumers do not fit the pattern at all. Many low-income households would gain from price changes, while many higher-income households face losses.

As rough as these estimates are, national average and median figures hide substantial variation across states in terms of toll call expenditures. Data from 1982 for the seven states served by Mountain Bell (Arizona, Colorado, Idaho, Montana, New Mexico, Utah, and Wyoming) show average residential toll bills of $19.00, which is close to the national average figures for 1983 and 1984. Iowa data from 1983, however, reveal average residential toll usage of much lower levels, only $10.00 per month. On the higher side, California data from 1983 show average monthly residential toll bills of $27.00. New York City average residential toll bills in 1986 are $19.00 for intrastate calls only, which would lead to *gains* in the repricing analysis of $4.00 per month for intrastate calls. Consumers in different states vary in their average toll usage and therefore in the incidence scenario they face.[19] In all states, however, median residential toll users face larger losses than the average.

The final question to be considered is how significant politically these losses of $0.00–$5.00 per month are to consumers, whether high or low income. The *maximum* $5.00 loss would have raised average local rates by between 33 percent and 50 percent depending on the state. One metric of comparison is actual telephone rate increases in the post-divestiture era. Local rates increased an average of about $3.00 from 1983 to 1986. In some states, such as Vermont and Wyoming, the increases approached $10.00 per month. From this perspective, $5.00 per month is a large increase. However, given that telephone expenditures average only about 2 percent of all household expenditures, a $5.00 rise for the hardest hit is not substantial relative to the entire household budget. Furthermore, a targeted lifeline program for needy low-income consumers can reduce the size of this loss.

Despite large local price increases in the early 1980s, average United States local telephone rates in 1986, about $14.14 per month, were still below the inflation-adjusted average rates of $14.99 as recently as 1976 and well below the $18.96 average in 1966. Factoring in the substantial cuts in toll rates after 1984, it becomes clear that the dynamic gains of technology led to greatly reduced toll rates in 1986 compared to 1976 and lower local rates as well, once inflation is taken into account. Adding in the second-order benefits of efficient pricing and competition improves the overall picture even further for residential telephone consumers.

GEOGRAPHIC BENEFITS AND COSTS

The monopoly structure of telecommunications markets under AT&T imposed several cross-subsidies. After divestiture, the Federal Communications Commission has reduced cross-subsidies under their jurisdiction, but some consumers still subsidized others on an interstate basis in the late 1980s.[20]

As shown in the previous section, residents of different states vary greatly in their propensity to use toll services. Since this analysis focuses on intrastate decision-making, however, the geographic costs and benefits will be assessed at the state level, between rural and urban consumers. Under the Bell monopoly, many state regulators priced local services based on the "value of service" concept, which held that subscribers in dense areas who could reach more other subscribers with a "free" local call paid more for local service because they were receiving more value. As a result, rural local telephone rates averaged $8.60 per month in 1982, while the overall national average was $10.18. Value of service pricing is irrelevant in an environment in which the prices of access and local calling are unbundled. Furthermore, the cross-subsidy to rural residents under value of service pricing is the opposite of pricing at cost, a policy under which access would be cheaper for subscribers in dense areas.

Even regulators who do not use "value of service" local pricing often average rates across their state to make tariffs simple and to fit notions of fairness. Since costs of access lines and toll calls vary based on distance to central office switches and the physical concentration of usage, urban consumers stand to benefit from deaveraged access prices while suburban and, particularly, rural consumers face losses.[21] Local operating company studies of the incremental costs of subscriber access by density zones find that access costs are substantially lower in dense areas and that there are economies of density in access. Studies estimating access costs can be disaggregated to the level of individual users rather than density zone, based on subscriber distance to the central office, but implementing this level of disaggregation may be more costly than the benefits would support.

New Jersey Bell estimated the incremental cost differences among four density zones in a range from $6.00 to $14.00 per month in 1984. A similar study in Wisconsin in 1984 estimated a range from $7.00 to $14.00 for incremental access costs per month. In Illinois, regulators implemented a policy to charge subscribers in Chicago only $3.00 per month for access, while those in the suburbs faced charges of $6.00–$10.00 and rural residents paid more. New York Telephone claims that embedded access costs (rather than incremental costs) varied by central office exchange area from $7.00 in the most dense parts of Manhattan to $30.00 in upstate areas in 1986.

Rural telephone companies have received significant subsidies for their capital costs from the federal Rural Electrification Administration. Most state regulators also have subsidized high-cost rural companies and residents substantially and explicitly by the sharing or "pooling" of intrastate toll revenues with urban companies. Rural access costs are extremely high for subscribers living far from switches. New technologies not requiring copper wire but instead using microwave systems for access may become more cost-effective, but, ironically, these new technologies will not become economically viable until regulators eliminate the cross-subsidy (Noll, 1986).

What does the potential removal of the cross-subsidy to rural consumers imply for the incidence issue? If the average *effective* local access charge (excluding local usage) is $5.00 in a state prior to deaveraging, then a range from $3.00 to $14.00 as implemented in Illinois, could mean an increase of up to $9.00 per month. A $9.00 monthly increase would be larger than the end-user access charge that the average state utility commission needs to eliminate completely the average access subsidy from intrastate toll prices. Thus, elimination of the urban/rural price differential to reflect costs would affect some groups more than *any* other policy change, which is why only one state (Illinois) had tackled it directly by 1989.

More finely tuned deaveraging would have had even more substantial implications for rural consumers, whose access lines can cost $50.00 per month or more. As with certain transportation services, it may be appropriate to subsidize rural consumers to allow them access to the services available in the rest of the nation and to allow the rest of the nation access to them. It is less clear what policy objective is served by subsidizing relatively affluent suburbanites from the pockets of urban dwellers.

INTEREST GROUP INCENTIVES

Most people in the game of state telecommunications regulation seem fairly well informed about the gain and loss scenario, particularly for themselves. With the complexities of telecommunications regulatory issues, however, no one has full information, not even the organizations with the most incentives. And information asymmetries do exist; regulated firms and large businesses know far better than regulators and legislators what their costs, markets, and future technologies hold.

Big businesses hold a large stake in telecommunications regulation, are easy to organize, and have other service options. Small businesses hold few of the same levers and do not appear to be large losers or winners in the deregulatory process. Only residential consumers making few toll calls face losses from deregulation but they probably will not lose enough to overcome the substantial barriers to sustained organization. It is difficult to imagine a grass-roots consumer response based on the monetary incentives identified in this chapter. Regulatory attempts to implement local measured service, however, have run into a "loss of free lunch" problem that has galvanized consumers. Regulators know that eliminating the subsidy to rural consumers causes the largest distributional changes and therefore regulators in only one state have reduced directly the rural access subsidy.

The large business users are very well organized politically and active in state regulatory proceedings. They are the type of businesses that Lindblom (1977) identifies as influential in the regulatory process merely because all other parties want to keep them on the system to help share fixed costs. They hold a powerful silent veto on many policy options. Large telecommunications-using firms are not silent, however, because of their interest in providing telecommunications services for themselves, whether for economic, technological, or privacy considerations. These firms depend on telecommunications services and devote substantial resources to them. As Travers Waltrip, vice president of the Travelers Companies, notes: "We do not make widgets but we do market financial instruments made through knowledge. We are totally dependent on people and information technology" (Teske, 1987, p. 12). Thus, these individual firms have every incentive to lobby actively in the regulatory process, and they do.

The several organizations representing large user interests, such as the Committee of Corporate Telecommunications Users (CCTU) and the New York Clearinghouse of Banks, participate actively in regulatory processes in major states. These are powerful interests who have the additional advantage of being able to use the decentralizing potential of telecommunications technology to threaten "voting with their feet." For the two major regulatory decisions that I analyze here, large users favor price changes and the opening of all markets to competition.

The incidence picture for small businesses adds to the standard organizational cost explanation (Olson, 1965) of why several small businesses are less likely to organize to oppose a policy change than a few large ones. The uneven distribution of toll-calling patterns of small businesses makes it very difficult for them to form political coalitions on telecommunications regulatory issues. As a group, it is not clear whether small businesses favor price changes, although they prefer competition not linked to price changes. Some existing small business organizations do not lobby actively on telecommunications issues, while others, such as the National Federation of Independent Business, have opposed specific FCC policies that seem to harm small businesses, including the $6.00 per line per month access charge for multiline subscribers.

This evidence explains why most small business associations are not active participants in state regulatory proceedings on price changes. Small business organizations played a role in registering complaints about service issues in the transitional period after divestiture. These firms do not have the same competitive options as large users, although equipment providers are developing smaller on-site switches; in addition, the expansion of shared tenant services in "intelligent buildings" will eventually increase the service options for small businesses. By 1990, however, the mixed monetary impacts provided no strong incentive to overcome barriers to organization.

Residential users are also divided into those who would gain from price changes and those who would lose. Although a substantial minority of consumers would gain, a majority of residential consumers face losses if and when regulators eliminate the various cross-subsidies. The large number of geographically dispersed consumers experiencing such small losses creates severe obstacles to overcoming the free rider and organizational cost problems. The large amount of publicity about the AT&T breakup, however, emphasizing its likely effect on local telephone rates, has helped focus consumer attention to some degree. And, because of previous efforts of political entrepreneurs, existing consumer groups lobby in favor of maintaining the old rate structure. Consumer groups favor competition, if it is not linked explicitly to price changes.

Residential interests are represented by both governmentally supported and nongovernmental consumer interest groups. The pre-existing governmentally supported advocates do not need to galvanize consumer interest to the same extent as grass-roots organizations. Some grass-roots groups, especially those representing elderly and rural consumers, participate in regulatory proceedings, often opposing local measured service. On the national level, the Consumer Federation of America, a coalition of consumer-interest groups, is very active in opposing price changes and in disseminating studies showing actual increases in local telephone rates.

Thus, the incidence of price changes explains much of the variation in the degree of organization, involvement, and activity of stakeholder groups. The intensity of consumer opposition to local measured service, however, is not explained well by economic impacts, as most would gain, but may require an explanation based in the consumer psychology of risk aversion and the loss of a perceived "free good." The analysis here suggests that regulators need not worry about the political impacts of price changes as much as they appear to, *if* they can take credit for toll rate declines as well as shouldering only some of the blame for the local increases. No doubt this is a difficult political task.

To complete the interest group scenario, I consider several other interests. The regulated firms hold the largest stakes in these decisions and thus the largest incentives to try to influence them. The local telephone companies favor rapid decisions about price changes so that competitive services can be offered at their economic cost, and slow decisions on competition, hoping that entrants will be allowed in only after price changes, according to a "level playing field" strategy.[22] These companies maintain large regulatory affairs staffs, control thousands of jobs in the states in which they operate, and have been active regulatory participants for 75 years.

As would be expected, potential entrants hold opposite interests to local telephone companies. These firms wish to compete in as many markets as possible to gain economies of scale and scope, and want to do so before local operating companies change their prices. While potential entrants are often portrayed as having little political clout, such is not the case in state telecommunications regulation. AT&T, US Sprint (backed by GTE), and MCI (backed by IBM) are large companies and well experienced in regulatory and antitrust battles. In addition, large users such as Citicorp, General Motors, and McDonnell Douglas, are potential competitors, as they provide substantial tele-

Table 4.2

Interest Group Positions Summary Chart

PRICE CHANGES	
Pro	Con
Operating Companies	Small Consumers
Large Users	Entrants

COMPETITION CHOICES	
Pro	Con
Entrants	Operating Companies
Large Users	
Small Consumers	

communications services for themselves and could sell excess capacity to outside firms. These companies have significant experience dealing with government regulators from other regulatory arenas and from their participation in the defense procurement process.

Thus, the likely impact of price changes and competition on different interest groups explains their incentives to support or oppose these policy choices. Given these differences in the magnitudes of impact and the degree of organization, we expect these groups to have different effects on regulatory policy. Table 4.2 summarizes the general interest group positions on pricing and competitive issues. The coalitions are more balanced for price changes than for choices about competitive entry.

5 Quantitative Analysis of State Decisions

States have responded differently to the changes in the telecommunications environment created by the AT&T breakup, the threat of local bypass, and the competitive possibilities created by the replacement of coaxial cable with microwave and fiber optical transmission. Some states have reduced toll prices closer to marginal costs and some also have permitted competitive entry into intrastate, intraLATA long distance markets. Other states have continued cross-subsidies for local service and have permitted the local Bell Operating Companies to maintain their monopoly in intrastate telephone service. What are the determinants of the variation in state regulation of telecommunications policy?

In this chapter I estimate two models of state telecommunications decisions to assess the relative effects of interest group preferences, contextual economic conditions, and institutional characteristics on policy outcomes. The results suggest that, while variables from each theory are important, the addition of bureaucratic and legislative factors helps to explain state choices far better than interest group preferences and contextual economic conditions alone.

METHODOLOGY

An unconstrained test of the theories outlined in Chapter 2 would combine cross-sectional and time-series data. It would use annual measures of the relevant concepts and pool them. The test would utilize a range of economic and technological data for each state, and detailed measures of the actual participation and strength of interest groups in regulatory proceedings. The researcher would interview regulators and their staff members in each state intensively about their attitudes toward telecommunications regulation. It would be an enormous undertaking to collect all the time-series data for all 50 states that would be required for such a test.

Given limited resources, I estimate two 50-state cross sections, one for pricing and one for competitive entry decisions in the period after divestiture. I use a logit regression technique to estimate the two models. Logit, a maximum likelihood estimator, is appropriate given a

63

binary dependent variable, where ordinary least square would be subject to heteroskedasticity.[1] I report the results for a one-stage logit analysis; however, to test whether two of the institutional variables used are endogenous, I compare these results to a two-stage model.

Dependent Variables

How can one compare the choices that states have made about telecommunications pricing given that each local telephone operating company provides several services, each with different prices? One possibility is the technique used by Kalt (1981) and Kalt and Zupan (1984). In their analyses of congressional energy decisions, they converted legislators' discrete voting choices into continuous measures of support for the positions favored by crude-oil and strip-mine owners. In this study I could have converted discrete state regulatory decisions into analogous continuous measures that ranked states according to their support for economic efficiency in pricing and entry. I choose not to utilize this procedure because opening markets to competition is an all-or-nothing decision that is not easily converted to a continuous measure. For pricing choices, it would be difficult and somewhat arbitrary to construct a ranking. As I am most interested in whether or not the regulators are moving towards economic efficiency in any way, a simple measure is preferred to a complicated, and perhaps indefensible, one.

Another possibility is to code state decisions as favoring or opposed to efficiency using a dichotomous measure. For example, several states passed deregulatory legislation between 1984 and 1987. Many of these laws, however, simply empowered public utility commissions to make deregulatory decisions, a power many did not legally hold, or addressed less controversial issues, like the detariffing of Centrex rates. Therefore, simple passage of a telecommunications deregulatory bill is not a useful proxy for state pricing policy favoring economic efficiency, our true variable of interest.

I have chosen to code state regulation as economically efficient if it either reduced intrastate toll rates or established an unbundled intrastate residential subscriber access charge. If a state pursued either of these policies after divestiture, it is coded as economically efficient in its *pricing decisions*. States that did not pursue such policies are scored as zero. These two criteria directly mirror Federal Communications Commission decisions after divestiture that reduced interstate long distance rates (by over 30 percent) and initiated a subscriber line charge ($3.50 on residential bills in 1989). Seventeen out of the 49 cases made these efficient pricing decisions between 1984 and 1987.[2]

Many services provided only by the local operating companies, including intraLATA toll, shared tenant services, Centrex, and pay telephones, may not be natural monopolies and may be provided competitively. I have chosen to use intraLATA competition as my indicator of a state's attitude towards entry issues, because intraLATA calls compose about one-fourth of the national toll call market and hence intraLATA toll competition has been the most important and controversial of the competitive choices faced by state regulators. IntraLATA competition allows firms other than the local operating company to complete calls within a metropolitan service area.[3] In the second regression, a state is assigned a 1 if facilities-based intraLATA *competition* was authorized and a 0 otherwise. Sixteen states approved facilities-based competitive entry into intraLATA markets between 1984 and 1987.

Table 5.1 summarizes the policy choices of the 48 states and the District of Columbia. Nearly one-half of the states (23) did not change prices or allow competitive entry during this period.

Table 5.1

State Policy Choices on Price Changes and Competitive Entry

Inertia	Don't Allow (0) Competition				Allow Competition (1)	
C P	AL	IND			ILL	MASS
H R	AZ	MICH			NY	ORG
A I (1)	CAL	ND			NM	PA
N C	DEL	UT			MY	
G E	VA	WY				
E S						
D C P	ARK	KN	NV	TN	FL	OH
O H R	COL	KT	NH	WV	IW	TX
N A I (0)	CN	ME	OK	WS	MN	VT
' N C	DC	MP	RI	NJ	MO	WA
T G E	GA	MT	SC	LA	NC	
E S	ID	NB	SD			

The simple correlation between pricing and competition choices is .24, and the adjusted *R*-squared from regressing one on the other is .01. Thus, they are not highly correlated decisions, suggesting that the choices are distinct and should be analyzed separately.

INDEPENDENT VARIABLES AND HYPOTHESES

In Chapter 2 I introduced the theories that scholars believe explain bureaucratic behavior. In this section, I develop measures of the relevant concepts for telecommunications interest groups, contextual variables, and institutional factors. The 11 independent variables are: large business users (FORT), grass-roots consumer advocacy (GA), government-funded consumer advocacy (PA), a dummy variable for the most aggressive regional holding company (USW), penetration of cable television (CATV), the interstate cross-subsidy flows (NECA), average access loop costs (LC), elected commissioners (EA), regulatory budgets (BUD), legislative party control (LEGP), and regulatory climate (RC).

Large businesses are the interest group with the most to gain from price changes and competition in telecommunications markets, because they are the predominant users of toll services. Since the intensity of geographic locations of large service-oriented companies is important, the proxy variable used is the number of headquarters of Fortune Service 450 firms in a given state. These Fortune 450 firms include the 100 largest diversified service companies, the 100 largest commercial banks, the 50 largest savings institutions, the 50 largest diversified financial companies, the 50 largest life insurance companies, the 50 largest transportation firms, and the 50 largest utility companies, matching the industries that exhibit high toll usage. The 50 largest retail trade firms included in the Fortune Service 500 listing are not included in this analysis because of the low average usage for that sector. Firm headquarters are used because they are the places from which a large amount of telecommunications traffic flows *and* because they carry political clout in states that care about the number of major firms headquartered in their domain. The hypothesis (hypothesis about interest groups, no. 1—H:I1) is that the presence of large users in a state increases the likelihood of both price changes and competition.

Lobbyists representing widely dispersed small consumers have become increasingly active in regulatory proceedings in the last 15 years. In some state telephone regulatory proceedings, grass-roots advocates have lobbied for the interests of elderly consumers, who presumably do not make large numbers of toll calls and depend on affordable local service; rural consumers, who face large increases in toll and access prices if deaveraging is allowed; and poor households, who fear that higher access costs will leave them without an affordable connection to the network. William Gormley (1983) characterizes the activity in public utility cases of grass-roots consumer advocates in the late 1970s across the fifty states as either high or low. Since it is not feasible to develop measures for consumer input specifically in telephone rate cases across all fifty states, I use the Gormley variables as bivariate proxies.

Consumers are also often represented by advocates funded by state governments. These advocates are generally better funded than grass-roots organizations, often based on a levy on the receipts of the utilities in the state. Both types of advocates oppose price changes but favor competition not linked to price changes. Gormley characterizes government-funded advocate activity in each state as well. The hypothesis (H:I2) is that in states where either or both kinds of consumer advocacy is strong, regulators are less likely to implement price changes and more likely to allow competitive entry.

The regulated companies themselves traditionally have been viewed as the most important interest group influencing regulatory decisions, starting with the capture theory and moving through Stigler's economic theory of regulation. Yet, all of the seven regional holding companies that control (as subsidiaries) the major telephone operating companies in the 50 states have similar interests in promoting price changes. Some companies express these interests more forcefully than others and some do not oppose competition but instead try to use its emergence in any form as justification for changing prices and eliminating cross-subsidies. Thus, while all regulated firms favor price changes, the expected position on competition depends on the firm and on related regulatory decisions.

The most vocal and prominent regional holding company by far has been U S West, which serves the western states other than California and Nevada. A front-page article in the September 24, 1987, *Wall Street Journal* said, "All seven regional Bells as well as their former parent, American Telephone and Telegraph Co., are pushing for further deregulation. But none is seeking it on the scale that U S West wants or has so irked regulators, legislators, and consumer groups" (Roberts, 1987). Four state regulators from states served by U S West subsidiaries agreed at an Aspen Institute conference that U S West is extraordinarily aggressive in its regulatory behavior (Teske, 1987). A dummy variable for the 14 states served by subsidiaries of U S West is included in the regression to determine if the holding company ownership makes a difference in achieving regulatory change, with other factors held constant. The hypothesis (H:I3) is that pressure by U S West makes politicians and bureaucrats in states served by U S West subsidiaries more likely to change prices and to allow competitive entry into intraLATA markets.

Cable television firms, as potential competitors for local telephone companies, are the final important interest group whose influence I analyze. The percentage of households served by cable television in a state measures their stake. The broadband video capability of the cable lines that enter households enables voice and data traffic to be carried to switches. Cable provides the most logical potential competitor for local telephone access loops. The problem of deterrence of new investment in the face of a possible natural monopoly is reduced by the fact that cable television lines are already sunk, both literally and figuratively, in the areas served (see Dixit, 1980). Thus, the hypothesis (H:I4) is that in states served by cable, regulators are less likely to make price changes and more likely to allow competition due to the political and economic strength of incumbent cable television firms. The data are from the 1986 *Metropolitan Statistical Data Book*, and the 1984 percentage of television households served by cable television ranges from 4 percent to 70 percent.

All regulators must respond to their economic environment to some extent when balancing the need for utility financial health and low consumer rates. Some important differences that regulators may consider are the interstate flow of cross-subsidies as mandated by the FCC and implemented by the National Exchange Carriers Association (NECA) and the average access loop costs in a state.

The mix of intrastate and interstate calling patterns may affect regulatory decisions. The interstate flow of NECA funds provides a proxy for calling patterns because funds flow mainly from low-cost, high interstate-use states to high-cost, low interstate-use states. In the 1990s, NECA interstate subsidies are being phased out, as regulators found them to be unfair. High-growth states, especially Florida and California, receive a large portion of the subsidy, even though they are not poor states. The data I use are 1984 National Exchange Carrier Association figures, with a range of a $190 million outflow from New Jersey to a $254 million subsidy into Florida. The hypothesis (H:C1) is that regulators in states with net outflows of funds are more likely to favor price changes and competitive entry because they are aware of the damage wrought by cross-subsidies, and states receiving subsidies that would be phased out could not easily also change prices under their own jurisdiction.

The density of a state's population may affect several elements of telephone regulation. Most important for this analysis is the fact that access loop costs are based largely on the distance to central office switches. Thus, in rural states access loops are longer and more expensive. As the federal pooling process administered under NECA reduces this cross-subsidy on an interstate basis, concomitant pressure is exerted on state regulators to eliminate the cross-subsidy. I use the 1983 average access loop costs in each state as reported by the FCC. The loop costs in the 48 states and Washington, D.C. range from $74.00 per year ($6.00 per month) in Washington, D.C. to $291.00 per year ($24.00 per month) in Wyoming. The hypothesis (H:C2) is that regulators in states with higher average access costs are more likely to change prices but less likely to allow competition, to give themselves time to adjust.

The four independent variables measuring institutional factors include those capturing regulatory structures and those capturing regulatory attitudes. Regulatory structures do not in and of themselves induce policy choices. They may affect the regulators' views of the problem, however, and the internal bureaucratic decision-making process. The variables I analyze include the election or appointment of commissioners and the budget for analyzing and implementing regulatory choices. I use a dummy variable for states with elections of regulatory commissioners. The hypothesis (H:RS1) is that elected commissioners are more likely to favor consumers' (that is, voters') short-term interests, by not changing price structures and by allowing competition.

The resources available may affect regulators' decisions because they allow for better analyses of the difficult policy choices. I use the full state public utility regulatory budget rather than a per capita budget figure because total analytic capability is the more relevant concept. Regulatory commission staffs include a small number of people who handle consumer complaints and monitor services. Larger states require more such staff. Nevertheless, most regulatory resources are devoted to policy analysis in one form or another, and, since a critical mass of analytic resources is required, the absolute budget is a better measure of analytic capacity. The National Association of Regulatory Utility Commissioners publishes state regulatory budgets. I use 1984 data, with a range from $1.2 million to $56 million. The hypothesis (H:RS2) is that regulators with higher budgets are more likely to change price structures and to allow competitive entry.

The attitudes of regulators and the politicians that review, and sometimes prescribe, their policies are important variables in the theoretical literature. Regulatory Research Associates (RRA) is a private firm devoted to assessing the regulatory climate in different state public utility commissions for utility stock analysts and shareholders. Unlike several Wall Street firms that also sell stock in these utilities, the RRA assessments have no obvious biases. Their 1985 assessments range from zero to nine, with a higher figure indicating a better climate for firms subject to regulation. Using this assessment as an independent variable is not equivalent to predicting policy changes by measuring actual changes because the regulatory climate assessment combines measures of commissioners' attitudes (from interviews) with past decisions across the whole spectrum of regulated industries, including the electricity, nuclear power, hazardous waste, natural gas, water and sewer, and telecommunications industries. The hypothesis (H:RA1) is that commissions with higher ratings are more likely to move telecommunications regulation into the new environment by changing prices and allowing competitive entry.

Since some legislatures have intervened in telecommunications regulatory decisions and others may have pressured regulators indirectly, their influence must be measured. My hypothesis (H:RA2) is that party control of the legislatures is likely to affect regulatory decisions; Republicans are more likely to favor the interests of the regulated firms by pushing for price changes and opposing competition, while Democrats are more likely to favor consumers by opposing price changes and allowing competition. States with both houses controlled by the Republicans are coded with a 1, states with mixed control are coded 0, and states with two Democratic houses are coded -1. The party control data are from the 1986 *Metropolitan Statistical Data Book* and are from 1985.[4]

Table 5.2 shows the relationships of the independent variables to be tested. Some of the simple correlation coefficients are fairly high, but most are not.

Table 5.2

Simple Correlations Between Independent Variables

	CATV	NECA	LC	PA	GA	FORT	USW	EA	LEGP	BUD	RC
CATV	1										
NECA	.10	1									
LC	.44	.47	1								
PA	-.15	-.27	-.28	1							
GA	-.31	-.04	-.32	.06	1						
FORT	-.17	-.01	-.34	.12	.26	1					
USW	.13	.22	.17	-.28	-.13	-.28	1				
EA	.06	.08	.34	-.19	-.31	.26	.20	1			
LEGP	.22	-.03	.09	.11	-.20	-.16	.46	-.02	1		
BUD	-.05	.15	-.15	.05	.12	.82	-.20	-.18	-.22	1	
RC	-.22	.14	-.32	.07	.26	.38	-.04	-.32	-.07	.24	1

The highest correlations are between the regulatory budget (BUD) and large users (FORT) at .82; between access loop costs (LC) and NECA subsidies at .47; between U S West and Republican legislatures at .46; and between access loop cost (LC) and cable television penetration (CATV) at .44.

RESULTS FOR PRICING DECISIONS

Table 5.3 shows the impact of each independent variable on pricing decisions in a single overall regression equation. Many of the variables are strongly and significantly related to state regulatory decisions. The regression as a whole is highly significant (98 percent), with two highly significant variables (95 percent or higher) and two more above 89 percent significance.

Three of the four variables in the institutional theory are strongly related to pricing decisions. A more highly rated regulatory climate and a larger budget for regulation strongly increase the likelihood of

Table 5.3

Effect of Eleven Independent Variables on Pricing Decisions

VARIABLE	THEORY	BETA	STD. E.	SGNF.	AAR.
Interest Groups					
Fortune 450 HQs	+	−0.09	0.10	66%	.71
Grass-roots Advocates	−	0.82	0.94	62%	.06
Government-Funded Advocates	−	0.20	0.88	18%	.05
U S West	+	0.94	1.05	63%	.20
Cable Television	−	−0.04	0.05	60%	.09
Contextual Variables					
NECA	−	−0.02	0.01	89%	.25
Access Loop Costs	+	0.01	0.02	55%	.41
Institutional Variables					
Elected Commissioners	−	1.36	1.09	79%	.08
Budget for Regulation	+	0.31	0.14	97%**	.67
Legislative Control	+	1.04	0.58	92%*	.15
Regulatory Climate	+	0.39	0.20	95%**	.13

Logit Chi-Square 22.7 (98 percent), N = 49

**greater than 95% significant.

*greater than 90% significant.

When this regression is run using ordinary least squares rather than logit, the adjusted R-squared value is .19, meaning that about one-fifth of the variation in state pricing choices is explained by the model, and the results for the individual variables are virtually unchanged.

The influence of Walker's Index will be analyzed separately later in this chapter.

decisions to change price structures, as hypothesized. States with Republican legislative control are also more likely to change prices, as expected. One contextual variable shows a strong relationship to pricing decisions. States with higher outflows of interstate NECA subsidy funds are more likely to change prices. None of the interest group variables shows a strong, significant relationship to decisions to change prices.

The other six independent variables are not highly significant, and half have coefficients with signs opposite the theoretical expectation, including the impact of elected regulatory commissioners.[5]

The predictive power of this model is very strong. States can be considered to be predicted accurately when the predicted value is .5 or higher and the state did actually implement the price change, or when the predicted value is .49 or lower and the state did not change prices. With this methodology, 42 of the 49 cases are predicted correctly, for 86 percent accuracy. Before estimating the model, we might have guessed zero for each of the 49 cases, and since the modal value of zero held in 65 percent of the cases, we would have achieved 65 percent accuracy. Thus, the model reduced the error in prediction by 60 percent (21 out of the 35 unexplained percentage points).

How strong are the effects of the individual independent variables? Table 5.4 shows the probability impact on decisions to change price structures of moving each variable from its lowest value (LV), to a standard deviation below the mean (SDBM), to a standard deviation above the mean (SDAM), to its highest value (HV), with the other variables evaluated at their means.

Some independent variables have very strong impacts on regulatory decisions to change prices. Based on a standard deviation departure from the mean in both directions, three institutional variables—the regulatory budget, the regulatory climate, and the legislative party control—have impacts of .3 or greater on the probability of a price change decision. A change in the budget from $1.2 million (one standard deviation below the mean) to $17.7 million (one standard deviation above the mean) leads to an 82 percent increase in the likelihood of a decision to change prices, with other variables evaluated at their means. Similarly, a change in the regulatory climate from 1.9 to 7.5 leads to a 38 percent increase in the likelihood of a decision in favor of changing prices.

One interest group variable (Fortune 450) and one contextual variable (NECA) also have large impacts on the probability of price changes. The three institutional variables and NECA are also the four most significant variables in the analysis (and Fortune 450 is not significant only because of the correlation with the regulatory budget).

Table 5.4

Marginal Effect of Each Variable with Other Variables Set at Their Means

	LV	SDBM	SDAM	HV	SDBM-SDAM CHANGE
Interest Groups					
Fortune 450 HQs	.41	.41	.09	.002	-.32*
Grass-roots Advocates	.17	.17	.31	.31	+.14
Government-Funded Advocates	.22	.22	.25	.25	+.03
U S West	.19	.19	.32	.38	+.13
Cable Television	.63	.32	.17	.11	-.15
Contextual Variables					
NECA	.93	.53	.08	.001	-.45*
Access Loop Costs	.11	.17	.32	.53	+.15
Institutional Variables					
Elected Commissioners	.17	.17	.37	.45	+.20
Budget for Regulations	.03	.03	.85	1.00	+.82**
Legislative Control	.13	.13	.43	.54	+.30*
Regulatory Climate	.05	.10	.48	.63	+.38*

**change greater than .50.
*change greater than .30.

When all variables are evaluated at their means, the probability of a price change decision is .28.

In similar studies of regulatory change, most previous scholars have analyzed the impact of interest group and contextual variables only, without giving proper attention to institutional factors. One way to identify just how important these institutional factors are is to compare the fully specified model with a model that includes only the interest group and contextual variables. The results for this latter model are presented in Table 5.5.

The seven-variable regression in Table 5.5 is much weaker than the full model presented in Table 5.3. The results for the regression are only significant at the 71 percent level. A nested chi-squared test rejects the null hypothesis that the full model from Table 5.3 is no better than this model at a 99 percent level if the additional four institutional variables increase the equation's chi-squared value by more than 13.3; the actual increase is 14.1, so the full model is a significantly improved specification.

Table 5.5

Effect of Seven Interest Group and Contextual Variables on Pricing
Decisions

VARIABLE	THEORY	BETA	STD. E.	SGNF.
Interest Groups				
Fortune 450 HQs	+	0.08	0.04	95%**
Grass-roots Advocates	–	0.11	0.73	12%
Government-Funded Advocates	–	0.13	0.76	14%
U S West	+	1.54	0.87	92%*
Cable Television	–	-0.03	0.04	54%
Contextual Variables				
NECA	–	-0.01	0.01	79%
Access Loop Costs	+	0.01	0.01	50%

N = 49
Logit Chi-Square 8.56 (71%)

**greater than 95% significant.
*greater than 90% significant.

Five of the seven variables in the model in Table 5.5 have
approximately the same, insignificant results as in the fully specified
model. Both the Fortune 450 and the U S West variables are now
significantly and positively associated with price changes, which
matches their theoretical expectations.[6] Even more important is that
when this seven-variable model is used for predictions, it proves to be
greatly inferior to the full model including institutional factors. Only
34 of the 49 pricing choices are predicted correctly by the model in
Table 5.5, which at 69 percent is only a marginal improvement over the
pre-regression modal prediction of no change in rate structures in 65
percent of the states. (Recall that the full model predicts 42 of the 49
cases accurately, for 86 percent). Furthermore, the decision to *change*
prices, far more than a decision to stay with the status quo, requires
an analysis of institutional factors. While the model including only
interest group and contextual variables predicts three states to
change prices that did not (of the 32 that did not), it fails to predict 12
states (of the 17) that did change prices. When the model is specified
fully, as in Table 5.3, the predictions are corrected for 6 of these 12
states that actually changed prices. Thus, by ignoring institutional
factors, previous scholars have misspecified the model of regulatory

choices across jurisdictions, especially for the most innovative states.

I, too, must consider whether my full model is properly specified, particularly whether it is appropriate to treat the two institutional variables, regulatory budget and regulatory climate, as exogenous in this cross-sectional analysis. It is plausible that some of the same factors that determine pricing and competitive entry choices, but are not measured and therefore are in the disturbance term of the equation in Table 5.3, also affect regulatory budgets and climates. If so, and the effect is in the same direction, then treating these factors as exogenous in a one-stage regression biases their impact upward (Achen, 1986).

To test for this I compare the results in Table 5.3 to a two-stage model, where budgets and climates are regressed on plausible exogenous variables (instruments) that may "cause" them, plus the other exogenous variable already in the one-stage model. Then, these "predicted" budgets and climates, now "purged" of a correlation with the disturbance term of the policy equation, are used in the second-stage regression to predict choices about pricing.

In the first stage, I regress budgets upon state populations and electricity generation in the state, which should affect the size of the regulatory budget (electricity is the largest industry regulated by the state public utility commissions). Regulatory climates are regressed upon the percent metropolitan population in the state, the party of the governor, the state's presidential vote in 1972 (a measure of "liberalism" often used by political scientists), the median income of the state in 1984, and the average ADA ratings for the United States senators in that state. The other exogenous variables from the one-stage regression are also included in these first-stage regressions to "purge" the estimated values of the endogenous variables of a correlation with the disturbance term of the second-stage equation. This two-stage system is identified in its rank and order conditions (Kmenta, 1986).

In the first stage, population and electricity are jointly highly significant explanatory variables for state budgets (at the 99.9 percent level for a joint F-test), leading to a first-stage adjusted R-squared value of .69.[7] None of the five instrumental variables for regulatory climate perform nearly so well; in a joint F-test they are not nearly significant. The adjusted R-squared in the first-stage equation for regulatory climate is only about 0.2. Thus, I have found good instrumental variables to "explain" regulatory budgets, but I cannot find good instruments for regulatory climates. I tested several other combinations of instrumental variables with no more success. Achen (1986) notes that sometimes it is nearly impossible to find appropriate instrumental variables.

The second-stage logit results for pricing choices, with regulatory budget treated as endogenous, are fairly similar to the first stage results. The impact of the regulatory budget is somewhat reduced, but it still has the strongest impact of any of the eleven variables.[8] A change in the budget from $1.2 million to $17.7 million per year—the standard deviation departures from the mean—now results in a 32 percent greater likelihood of a decision to change prices, with other variables set at their means.[9]

Therefore, since the two-stage results are similar for the endogenous budget, and I cannot generate a reasonable first-stage model for regulatory climate, I will continue to discuss the one-stage results in the rest of this analysis. The fact that these variables have strong impacts on regulatory choices is more important than the exact magnitude of the effect. The two-stage pricing results suggest that budgets, even treated as endogenous, remain the most important explanatory variable. Thus, I will discuss the one-stage results throughout, but I will temper the results for regulatory climate and limit policy prescriptions based on its impact.

RESULTS FOR COMPETITIVE ENTRY DECISIONS

Table 5.6 shows the impact of each independent variable on competition decisions in a single overall (one-stage) regression equation. Many of the variables are strongly related to state choices. The regression as a whole explains choices about competitive entry very well. It is significant at the highest levels and several independent variables are highly significant.

Three variables confirm the importance of interest groups (two of which are highly significant, while the other is almost significant). Regulators in states served by U S West subsidiaries are much more likely than others to approve competition. Regulators in states where government-funded consumer advocates are active are also more likely to approve competition. Regulators in states with more Fortune Service 450 headquarters are more likely to approve competition. No contextual variables show any strong or significant relationship to competition choices.

Two variables also confirm the importance of institutional factors: regulatory climate and party control of the legislature. Legislatures controlled by Democrats are much more likely to favor competitive entry, while more highly rated regulatory climates are also associated with a higher chance of competition. Whether or not commissioners are elected or appointed may also be important, but the evidence suggests that elected commissioners are less likely to favor competitive entry (which is contrary to my hypothesis).

Table 5.6

Effect of Eleven Independent Variables on Competition Decisions

VARIABLE	THEORY	BETA	STD. E.	SGNF.
Interest Groups				
Fortune 450 HQs	+	0.15	0.12	80%
Grass-roots Advocates	+	-0.49	1.44	26%
Government-Funded Advocates	+	5.63	2.74	96%**
U S West	+	8.40	3.92	97%**
Cable Television	+	0.06	0.07	62%
Contextual Variables				
NECA	–	-0.01	0.01	54%
Access Loop Costs	–	-0.01	0.03	34%
Institutional Variables				
Elected Commissioners	+	-4.56	3.05	87%
Budget for Regulation	+	-0.08	0.10	55%
Legislative Control	–	-3.53	1.49	98%**
Regulatory Climate	+	0.55	0.34	89%

N = 49
Logit Chi-Square 38.0 (99%)

**greater than 95% significant.
*greater than 90% significant.

The ordinary least squares version of this regression has an adjusted R-squared value of .39, which means that about two-fifths of the variance in state competition decisions is explained by the model.

The competition regression model predicts even better than the regression for decisions to change prices; 44 of the 49 cases are predicted correctly, for 90 percent accuracy. Since the modal choice is 69 percent "no competitive entry," the model reduces the error in prediction by 68 percent (21 out of the 31 unexplained percentage points).

How strong are these significant relationships? The strength of the relationships in the competition model is presented in Table 5.7.

Based on a standard deviation departure from the mean value, the U S West companies, government-funded advocates, and the legislative party control have the strongest impacts on competition policy choices, with increases over .5 in the likelihood of positive decisions. With other variables evaluated at their means, for example, a shift in both state legislative houses from Republican to Democratic would

Table 5.7

Marginal Effect of Each Variable with Other Variables Set at Their Means

	LV	SDBM	SDAM	HV	SDBM-SDAM CHANGE
Interest Groups					
Fortune 450 HQs	.02	.02	.41	.99	+.39*
Grass-roots Advocates	.11	.11	.07	.07	-.04
Government-Funded Advocates	.01	.01	.60	.60	+.59**
U S West	.01	.01	.82	.97	+.81**
Cable Television	.01	.05	.15	.28	+.10
Contextual Variables					
NECA	.38	.15	.05	.01	-.10
Access Loop Costs	.19	.13	.06	.03	-.07
Institutional Variables					
Elected Commissioners	.26	.26	.01	.01	-.25
Budget for Regulation	.16	.16	.04	.002	-.12
Legislative Control	.56	.56	.01	.001	-.55**
Regulatory Climate	.01	.02	.31	.51	+.29

**change greater than .50.
*change greater than .30.

The model predicts a .09 probability of competition being allowed, with all variables evaluated at their mean value.

mean an increase of 55 percent in the likelihood of a positive choice on competition. The effect of U S West is even greater; with other factors held constant, pressure by U S West increased the likelihood of competition choices by 96 percent. The presence of large users also has an important impact, increasing the probability of competition choices by 39 percent.

As with the analysis of decisions to change price structures, the effects of institutional factors can be highlighted by comparing the fully specified model in Table 5.6 with one including only the interest group and contextual variables. How does the fully specified competition regression model perform compared to a model used more often in the literature that includes only interest group and contextual pressures on regulators? As Table 5.8 shows, the results of this partial model are much stronger for competition than they were for price changes decisions (compare to Table 5.5). Nevertheless, the seven variable model does not perform nearly so well as the full competition model, with all eleven variables. A nested chi-squared test shows that the full model in Table 5.6 is significantly better than this model at the highest (99.9 percent) confidence levels.

Table 5.8

Effect of Seven Interest Group and Contextual Variables on Competition Decisions

VARIABLE	THEORY	BETA	STD. E.	SGNF.
Interest Groups				
Fortune 450 HQs	+	0.07	0.04	92%*
Grass-roots Advocates	+	0.55	0.82	50%
Government-Funded Advocates	+	1.98	0.94	96%**
U S West	+	2.03	1.07	94%*
Cable Television	+	0.01	0.04	07%
Contextual Variables				
NECA	–	0.00	0.01	08%
Access Loop Costs	–	-0.01	0.02	53%

N = 49

Logit Chi-Square 15.12 (96%)

**greater than 95% significant.
*greater than 90% significant.

As in the full model, activity by government-funded advocates and U S West subsidiaries are highly significant explanatory factors. All of the individual variable results are similar to those in the full competition model.

How well does the model in Table 5.8 predict choices about competitive entry? It correctly predicts only 36 of the 49 cases, for 73 percent accuracy, in contrast to the full model's 44 of 49 prediction, or 90 percent accuracy. This 73 percent accuracy is only a small improvement on the modal distribution of 69 percent of cases not allowing competitive entry.

The partial model in Table 5.8 predicts four states to allow competition that actually did not (out of 33 such states), but fails to predict nine (of the 16) states that actually did allow competition. As with price change decisions, institutional factors are even more necessary to explain the more innovative state decisions.

Even when some interest group preferences strongly influence telecommunications regulatory outcomes, predictions are greatly improved by analyzing institutional variables. For competition choices the seven-variable model performs far better than the same model explaining decisions to change prices, but its explanatory and predictive power is still substantially improved by the inclusion of institutional and attitudinal information in the full model. We can not fully understand state regulatory decisions that allow competitive entry into telecommunications markets and change prices without analyzing institutional factors.

Walker's Index

In Chapter 2 I discussed previous scholars' attempts to explain state policy innovation, particularly Walker's Index, a 1969 aggregate of state innovations. While Walker's Index bears a relationship to telecommunications policy choices, it does not explain them very well, and certainly not so well as the other models in this chapter. Testing Walker's Index alone yields a 96 percent significant relationship to price change decisions and a 94 percent significant relationship to competition choices. The overall explanatory power of the models is weak, however, as the ordinary least squares version of the regression shows adjusted R-squared values of .07 and .06, respectively. In comparison, two of the best variables from the models do somewhat better by themselves. The regulatory budget alone yields an adjusted R-squared value of .14 for pricing decisions and the legislative party control variable alone yields an adjusted R-squared value of .08 for competition decisions. Walker's Index is a significant explanatory variable but it does not perform better than more specific telecommunications regulatory variables.

Furthermore, when it is included in the two regression models with the other eleven variables, the independent impact of Walker's Index is not nearly significant. It is highly correlated with several other independent variables, including average loop costs (-.63), Fortune 450 headquarters (.57), regulatory budgets (.48), and elected commissioners (-.46), suggesting that Walker's Index captures elements of state size and population density. When some of these highly correlated variables are dropped out of the models (to enable estimation of the model), the independent impact of Walker's Index is still not significant, and the regressions as a whole are less strong.

Thus, Walker's Index relates significantly in predictable ways to innovative decisions to change telephone prices and allow competition, but it is not by itself a strong explanatory factor and it does not contribute to an improvement in the models. State telecommunications regulatory choices *are* related to state policy innovation more generally. An index developed 15 years before divestiture, however, is not an adequate explanatory factor for telecommunications choices in the 1980s. A focus on more specific variables expected to affect telecommunications regulatory choices is more fruitful in explaining state policy variation.

INTERPRETATIONS

Institutional factors are essential to a full explanation of state regulatory choices. The predictive power of the price change and competition regression is vastly improved when institutional variables are taken into account. Without the institutional factors, the interest group and contextual variables barely predict better than using the modal dependent variable value.

In a comparison of institutional factors versus interest group variables, institutional factors have a greater influence on telecommunications regulatory choices. More of the hypotheses regarding institutional variables are confirmed than are those for interest group variables. For the pricing decisions, the three most significant variables, regulatory budget, regulatory climate and legislative party control, are institutional explanations, and two of the three most potent explanatory variables are the budget and the regulatory climate. For competitive entry choices, the activity of government-funded advocates and U S West subsidiaries are significant, but so too are legislative party control, regulatory climate and appointment of commissioners. Legislative party control is the third most potent explanation of competition policy choices. Table 5.9 summarizes the confirmation of hypotheses.

My interpretation is that interest groups are important but when strong interest groups compete on both sides of complex issues, institutional factors are likely to explain more of the variance in decision-making. Interest groups are relatively more important in competition choices than in pricing because more groups favor competition not linked to price changes. Government-funded consumer advocates, for example, influence decisions about competitive entry but not decisions to restructure prices. Some interest groups variables, including large users and U S West, affect both pricing and competitive choices.

Of the interest group hypotheses, the expectations about the impact of the large business users are confirmed, although the collinearity with the regulatory budget in the full model for pricing decisions confounds the effect. Populous states have more Fortune Service 450

Table 5.9

Hypotheses Confirmed for Price and Competition Choices

	PRICE	COMPETITION
Interest Groups		
H: I1 Large Businesses	YES*	YES
H: I2 Consumer Groups	both insignificant	YES for Government advocates only
H: I3 U S West	insignificant**	YES
H: I4 Cable Television	insignificant	insignificant
Contextual Variables		
H:C1 NECA Subsidies	YES	insignificant
H:C2 Access Loop Costs	insignificant	insignificant
Institutional Variables		
H: RS1 Elected Commissioners	insignificant	NO, nearly significant but in wrong direction
H: RS2 Regulatory Budget	YES	insignificant
H: RA1 Regulatory Climate	YES	YES
H: RA2 Legislative Party Control	YES	YES

*without the budget variable, Fortune 450 HQs is significant and positive.
**without legislative party, U S West is significant in the interest group and contextual variable model.

headquarters and higher regulatory budgets, although these correlations are not nearly 1.00. Large states are more likely to make price changes and to allow competitive entry because of the combination of these two variables *and* the increased pressure applied by long distance companies such as AT&T, MCI, and US Sprint in the more populous markets.

The Gormley consumer advocacy measures are not important or significant variables in the analysis, with the exception of government-funded advocates' increasing the likelihood of competition. I believe that more detailed and updated measures of the strength of consumer advocacy would have more impact. Even with better measures, government-funded advocates probably have more influence on decisions than grass-roots advocates because their funding is assured by government and they do not need to arouse the public sentiment and support that grass-roots advocates require. As I suggested in Chapter 4, the losses from changing telephone prices are probably insufficient to motivate dispersed consumers to overcome the barriers to collective action.

The multivariate analyses confirm the anecdotal evidence that different political tactics in U S West states led to different regulatory results. U S West subsidiaries are significant factors in encouraging competition, because of their positive attitude towards open telecommunications markets. States served by U S West subsidiaries are 96 percent more likely to allow competition and 19 percent more likely to change prices.

Despite this mixed success, the interest group explanation performs far better than the contextual variable explanation, suggesting that regulators are more sensitive to interest group pressure than to existing economic, demographic, and technological differences in their states. The only confirmed hypothesis about contextual factors is that regulators respond to the flow of interstate subsidies. Regulators from states that subsidize other states' consumers are more likely to change prices and reduce cross-subsidies in their own domains. The coefficient for access loop costs has the expected sign, but is not significant.

The regulatory structure hypotheses show mixed results. Elected commissioners make significantly different choices for competition than appointed ones, and different pricing choices as well. In both cases, however, the impacts are in the unexpected direction. These results suggest that elected commissioners favor the interests of the local operating companies more than appointed ones, and are not so sensitive to short-run consumer interests as normally assumed. Perhaps part of the reason scholars find conflicting results for this variable is that elected commissioners may have reasons to favor other interests besides consumers. Electoral support can come in many forms, not merely votes, and commissioners may seek it from businesses as well as consumers.

The regulatory budget is the most potent explanatory variable and the most highly significant in decisions to change prices.[10] This confirms my expectation that larger staffs more fully analyze regulatory choices and find more reasons to change prices than to maintain the status quo. The budget variable does not significantly influence competition choices.

The hypothesis for the regulatory climate is confirmed in both models, showing that state telecommunications regulatory decisions are consistent with regulators' general policy attitudes and their decisions in other regulatory arenas. Better regulatory climates, as measured by Wall Street, lead to more innovative policy choices, in both pricing and competition.[11] This finding suggests that regulatory climate measures may be good measures of ideology, as constrained by constituents, similar to ADA ratings for congressmen.

The confirmation of hypotheses about legislative party control is important. A change in legislative control from Democratic to Republican, on average, leads to a 41 percent increase in the likelihood of a price change decision and a 55 percent decrease in the likelihood of a choice favoring competition. State legislative party activity parallels that at the federal level, where, in 1984, to aid small consumers the Democratic House passed a bill preventing the FCC from implementing subscriber line access charges while the Republican Senate considered but did not pass such a bill. Thus, while William Gormley and others suggested that legislators hold little incentive to intervene in these "zero-sum" regulatory battles, it is clear that regulators do take heed of legislative views at the state as well as federal level.

CONCLUSIONS

Regulators, their staff, and state legislators account for much of the variation in state policy choices that I have explained, in predictable and measurable ways. Incorporating these institutional explanations of regulatory change makes much stronger models than using only the simple, interest group pressure explanations. Predictions are vastly improved when institutional variables are included; without them, predictions are barely better than the modal value, and innovative states in particular are predicted badly. Telecommunications regulatory choices are not merely a function of interest group pressure and contextual variables.

These results support theories that emphasize the importance of internal, bureaucratic factors in regulation, such as Derthick and Quirk's (1985) explanation of how federal deregulation of airlines, trucking and telecommunications began at the bureaucratic staff level; and Meier's (1988) explanations of state insurance regulation. I believe it is the quasi-pluralist nature of interest group pressure in the contemporary environment that forces a closer look inside the regulatory bodies.

We might expect regulators to decide related issues in similar ways, but the evidence here seems to suggest that regulators are not so consistent. The puzzle is that price and competition choices should be more closely related than they are in the 49 cases presented (see Table 5.1). While they share some explanatory factors, different factors influence the choices about pricing and competitive entry. Choices about competitive entry are not related at all to any of the contextual variables. They are more related to interest group factors than are the decisions to change prices.

Why are pricing and competition choices not more closely linked? One possibility is that regulators use competitive entry more as a symbolic policy choice to respond to external pressure, but do not expect it to materialize in the near future to threaten existing cross-subsidies.[12] Price changes, on the other hand, are more substantial policy choices that more accurately reflect regulatory climates and attitudes. Price changes immediately harm large numbers of consumers, who can easily trace the change to regulators.

Furthermore, I believe interest groups are more influential in competition choices than in price change decisions because most of them favor the notion of competition when it is not linked directly to price changes. The interest group environment more clearly favors competition; therefore interest groups are more powerful. This confirms my theoretical expectation posited in Chapter 2. The crucial finding, however, is that price and competition choices are viewed and made separately in many states; when they are linked explicitly, more interest groups will oppose competitive entry, especially consumer groups.

The fully specified models predict state choices quite well, with only seven of 49 cases predicted wrong for decisions about price structures and five predicted incorrectly for competition choices. New Jersey is the only state that *both* models predict incorrectly. It is predicted to change prices and to allow competitive entry. It did neither. It is also the *only* state predicted to change prices that did not. I turn now to an intensive analysis of New Jersey in contrast to New York, which acted as the models predicted by changing prices and allowing competitive entry.

6 Comparative Case Study: New Jersey and New York

The quantitative models in Chapter 5 suggest that New Jersey should have made economically informed decisions about pricing and competitive entry. It has made neither; as we have seen New Jersey was the only state predicted inaccurately for choices about both pricing and competitive entry. Adding to this puzzle is New Jersey's tradition as a leader in telecommunications technology. New Jersey has long been the home of Bell Labs, and is now home to AT&T Labs, Bell Communications Research, AT&T International headquarters, and the National Exchange Carriers Association. New Jersey also has a tradition of innovation in other policy areas, ranking fourth in Walker's 1969 Index of innovation (New York was first). What, then, might account for the inaccurate prediction? In this chapter I shall explore decision-making in New Jersey to determine whether New Jersey is truly aberrant or whether other variables should be included in the models. I compare decision-making in New Jersey to that in New York. New York's decisions are predicted to be similar to New Jersey's, and in New York the predictions match actual choices. This comparison is based on participant observation, interviews with key actors, and review of all relevant documents, hearings testimony, and secondary sources.[1]

The different policy choices in the two states have led to different rates for telephone users. In 1985, the average New York Telephone customer paid $17.00 per month for local access and usage charges. The average 1985 New Jersey Bell local charge was $8.00 for flat-rate residential service. Thus, New York residents paid about two times as much for local service as New Jersey residents. Residential consumers in both states spent about the same amount, $14.00 per month, for other intrastate services, including intrastate toll calls and added services like touch-tone or call-forwarding.

Neither New York nor New Jersey residents paid the full embedded costs of local service in 1985. New York residents paid about 65 percent of local costs while New Jersey residents only paid 37 percent. After divestiture, this difference grew, as the percentage of local cost coverage increased 16 percent in New York from 1983 through 1986, but only 2 percent in New Jersey over the same period.

MULTIVARIATE COMPARISON

Both New Jersey and New York are large, northeastern states with advanced industrial and service economies, and both were among the first to regulate utilities starting nearly 80 years ago. Table 6.1 shows the values of independent variables from the multivariate analysis; they differ particularly in the institutional domain.

Table 6.1

Independent Variable Comparison—New Jersey and New York

	NEW JERSEY	NEW YORK
Interest Groups		
Fortune 450 HQs	17	60
Government-Funded Advocacy	1	1
Grass-roots Advocacy	0	1
U S West	0	0
CATV	57	38
Contextual Variables		
NECA Flows	-190	-100
Average Access Costs	122	141
Institutional Variables		
Elected Commissioners	0	0
Budget for Regulation	10	31
Regulatory Climate	5	8
Legislative Party	0	0

The two states differ somewhat on the interest group and contextual independent variables. New Jersey is the most densely populated state in the nation; consequently its average access costs are quite low. The figure used in the multivariate analysis is $122.00 per year. It is a largely suburban state with New York City dominating the northern area's economy and Philadelphia dominating the southern portion, thus prompting Benjamin Franklin to characterize the state as "a barrel with taps at both ends." New Jersey's economy has been very strong in the 1980s, with particular strength in services and pharmaceuticals. Although its large businesses are not concentrated in one major city, New Jersey has 17 Fortune Service 450 headquarters, which places it seventh in the nation.

New York is the second most populous state in the nation. The state's population is divided between the largest metropolitan area in the country, New York City and its suburbs, which comprise the downstate region; and a more rural upstate region. As a result, while the average access charges used in the quantitative analysis are $141.00 per year, they vary from $84.00 in downtown Manhattan to $360.00 in upstate Osceola.

In recent years the state, and particularly New York City, has lost employment to other jurisdictions, but New York City still has an extremely large concentration of major telecommunications-using businesses, particularly large financial firms. New York State has 60 Fortune Service 450 headquarters, second only to California. Several of these large firms had already established private microwave communication facilities prior to the AT&T divestiture, so much so that the ensuing congestion created the need for an underground fiber optic link to a Teleport on Staten Island.

In addition, the National Exchange Carriers Association interstate subsidy took more funds out of New Jersey than from any other state, in total and per capita. In 1984, a total of $190 million flowed out of New Jersey, while New York consumers lost $100 million. Cable television penetration in New Jersey exceeds that in New York, because most of New York City is still not wired for cable television by 1990. Fifty-seven percent of New Jersey television households received cable in 1984, compared to only 38 percent of New York television households.

Consumer advocacy by government-funded organizations is characterized as high in both states by Gormley (1983). Advocacy by grass-roots consumer groups is characterized as high in New York but not in New Jersey. In New Jersey small consumers are represented by the Public Advocate's Office, the first established in the nation. The Public Advocate relies on the Deputy Attorney General's Office for staff and legal support, and it has been active in telephone rate cases. Consumer interests are represented in New York by the state-funded Consumer Protection Board, which has been headed by Richard Kessel since 1984 with Governor Cuomo's strong support. Although the Shoreham nuclear power plant on Long Island has received its greatest attention in recent years, the Consumer Protection Board participates actively in all major telecommunications proceedings after divestiture.

Neither state is served by U S West subsidiaries. New Jersey Bell is a subsidiary of Bell Atlantic and New York Telephone is a subsidiary of NYNEX.

The two states differ on two of the four institutional variables. New Jersey's 1984 regulatory budget was about one-third the size of

New York's despite the fact that New Jersey's population is 40 percent as large as New York's. Regulatory Research Associates gave New Jersey an "average" rating of 5 for regulatory climate in 1985, while they gave New York's regulatory climate an "above average" rating of 8. Higher regulatory climate ratings, as we have seen, are associated with policy innovation.

In both states the legislative party control is mixed. Traditionally in New York, the Senate is Republican and the Assembly is Democratic; in New Jersey the situation is generally the opposite. Regulators are appointed by governors in both states, and confirmed by the state Senates rather than being elected by voters.

In the regression models, both states are predicted to change rate structures and to allow competition. The predictions are very high for New York, .99 for both choices, and nearly as high for New Jersey, .75 and .94 for price change and competition choices, respectively. Only six states, including New York, are predicted higher than New Jersey for rate structure decisions and only seven states are predicted higher for competition choices. The predictions for New York are on target; those for New Jersey are thoroughly wrong.

ACTUAL POLICY CHOICES

The two states made quite different telecommunications policy choices in the three years after divestiture. New Jersey regulators fought to keep local rates low and did not allow intraLATA competition, while the New York public service commission decreased toll rates and allowed intraLATA competition. This section compares in detail the policy choices made, first in New Jersey, then in New York.

New Jersey

New Jersey regulators increased intrastate toll rates rather than raising local rates, did not allow intraLATA competition, did not unbundle access from usage, and did not deaverage any rates. No intraLATA competition will be allowed until the Board of Public Utilities is convinced that basic rates or universal service are not threatened. Regulators handled Centrex, private lines, pay telephones, and other issues in a more pragmatic fashion, allowing more competition and local operating company flexibility when pushed by market considerations. In 1987, in response to the 1986 federal Tax Reform Act, the Public Advocate's Office negotiated a rate increase moratorium agreement with New Jersey Bell.

New Jersey has not allowed large rate increases and has not targeted those increases to local access rates. In a 1983 rate case, regulators awarded New Jersey Bell $41.5 million of a $216 million request, expanded local calling options for consumers, and increased local rates by $.15 per month. In 1985, the Board of Public Utilities allowed $94 million of a requested $300 million, in a case that involved New Jersey Bell, the Public Advocate and the board's staff. Private line services that were substantially underpriced prior to divestiture received $26 million of the $94 million increase. The other services to which rate increases were applied included $18 million for directory assistance charges, $11 million for operator service charges, $9 million for line connection charges, and $4 million for coin telephone service increases. The stipulation agreed to keep residential local service priced residually, after regulators increased other service prices. As a result, local rates received a $21 million increase, about $.45 per household per month, which kept New Jersey's local rates at or near the lowest in the nation.

In these rate cases New Jersey regulators approved only 26 percent of New Jersey Bell rate increase requests. They increased private line services, as well as "user charges" for directory assistance and other special services, rather than enact local residential increases. This policy was consistent with prior regulation in New Jersey when the average residential flat rate rose only 47 percent from 1972 to 1984, while the national consumer price index grew 161 percent over that period. The board did not reduce toll rates despite New Jersey Bell cost studies showing prices to be five times incremental costs and twice embedded costs.

The Board of Public Utilities did not hold any generic proceedings, as New York regulators did. Generally, the board reacted to requests by New Jersey Bell rather than initiating action. In 1987, New Jersey Bell proposed the three-year local rate increase moratorium, associated with the expected reduction in federal tax liability, in exchange for reduced regulation on more competitive services. The board accepted this deal.

The high population density in New Jersey allowed low local rates to be maintained, although the $8.00 monthly flat rate (including an average of about $4.00 in "free" usage) was well below the 1984 estimated $12.00 average long-run incremental costs of access alone. When broken down by four density zones across the state, incremental access costs varied from $6.00 to $14.00 per month. New Jersey Bell also had a very efficient network and claimed to have the fifth lowest intrastate toll rates in the nation in 1983, despite toll rates set at five times incremental costs.

New York

In contrast to New Jersey, when AT&T and the U.S. Department of Justice struck the Consent Decree in 1982, New York regulators had already reduced local message rates and intrastate toll rates in Cases 27995 and 28264 in the early 1980s, continuing the pattern from the 1970s rate cases under Alfred Kahn. Approved rate increases in these two cases, plus increases approved in Case 28601 in 1984 and Case 28961 in 1985 and 1986, totaled $1.4 billion. New York regulators approved 36 percent of the $3.95 billion requested (Economics and Technology, Inc., 1987), compared to 26 percent in New Jersey over the same time period.

The New York Public Service Commission relied heavily on "generic proceedings" in the post-divestiture period. Generic hearings focus on a particular issue of concern to regulators outside of rate increase hearings. Unlike rate increase hearings, generic proceedings are unlimited in time, and need not culminate in any decision. Alfred Kahn used these hearings to examine rate design and marginal cost pricing during his tenure at the commission in the 1970s, outside of the more politicized context of a rate case.

In 1983 the commission initiated Case 28710 to examine the "bypass" threat; in 1985 the commission, convinced that the bypass threat was real, ordered reductions in carrier access charges and intraLATA toll rates to reduce the economic incentives to bypass. The commission started a generic rate structure proceeding in 1984 that continued into 1987. The decision implemented a deaveraged Regional Call Plan for the New York metropolitan area and reductions in private line rates for large businesses. Regulators also approved a lifeline program in 1987 that allowed the 1.2 million poorest households of the state to receive significant reductions in installation charges and monthly local service rates. This approach recognized that a narrowly targeted subsidy is more economically efficient than a broad cross-subsidy to all local subscribers.

The regulators' decision in Case 28425, started in 1983, allowed intraLATA competition but required that carriers pay charges similar to those assessed for interLATA competition. To make the competition fair, however, the regulators required New York Telephone to assess itself the same charges. New York is one of only five states to have truly leveled the playing field for intraLATA competition in this manner.

The commission's decision in Case 28961, a 1985 general rate case, reflected the generic proceeding findings. Regulators raised local rates, an average of 3 percent, while they reduced intraLATA toll and carrier access charges by 14–27 percent.

The commission and New York Telephone agreed to an 18-month rate increase moratorium in 1985 in exchange for automatic increases for Federal Communications Commission changes in separations accounting and depreciation, or wage and tax increases. With the passage of the 1986 federal Tax Reform Act, however, New York

Telephone's federal tax liabilities fell greatly. Thus, Governor Cuomo and the state Consumer Protection Board negotiated a four-year extension to the moratorium, with a rate decrease in 1987. After extensive publicity of this event, the commission took the role of specifying and ratifying the deal. The moratorium agreement also included a new approach to regulation, *incentive regulation*, to give New York Telephone an incentive to cut costs and increase productivity. Regulators allowed them to keep one-half of any profits earned above the 14 percent target rate of return.

Thus, in the post-divestiture period the New York commission allowed fairly large total rate increases, but continued to reduce toll rates and raise local end-user access charges. Regulators did not prohibit intraLATA competition and made the competition more fair than in all but four other states. Divestiture shocked New Yorkers less than those in many other states, because regulators had begun to restructure rates ten years earlier, at Alfred Kahn's insistence. New York's high levels of penetration of local measured service, 66 percent of residences and 97 percent of businesses statewide, also contributed to an easier adjustment to efficient pricing.

REGULATORY AGENCIES AND THE POLICY PROCESS

There are important differences between New York's and New Jersey's historical approach to regulation, the regulatory staff responses and analysis, and the views and approaches of the regulators themselves. I discuss each of these factors and consider their role in the decision-making process.

The New Jersey Board of Public Utilities consists of three commissioners, no more than two from the same party, who serve overlapping six-year terms as appointed by the governor and confirmed by the Senate. The New York Public Service Commission is larger, with seven commissioners, no more than four representing a single party, also appointed to six-year overlapping terms by the governor, with Senate approval. Neither set of regulators has been subject to substantial input from the state legislature in telecommunications regulation, as regulators have been in many western and midwestern states.

The New Jersey Board of Public Utilities has not been dominated by a seminal figure in the 1980s. The commissioners after divestiture included President Barbara Curran, a Republican lawyer who served in the state Assembly and was on the board since 1980; George Barbour, a Democratic lawyer with Assembly experience who served with the board since 1976; and Robert Guido, a Republican actuary appointed in 1985. Though not an innovator, Barbour did have national exposure, serving as president of the National Association of Regulatory Utility Commission (NARUC) in 1986.

During the period of changes in telecommunications regulation, New York regulators and their staff have been influenced greatly by the effects of the 1974–1977 chairmanship of Alfred Kahn, the man who became most associated with deregulation in the United States (McCraw, 1984). Kahn's predecessor, Joseph Swidler, was also a national regulatory figure, having served under President Kennedy as chair of the Federal Power Commission. Still, Kahn was even more influential in New York.

While Kahn focused his attention on energy issues during the post-Arab oil embargo crises, his development of staff interest in marginal cost pricing and sophisticated industrial organization economics led to changes in telecommunications (Anderson, 1981).[2] In fact, New York regulators moved to change the structure of telephone prices in the late 1970s, not because of threatened bypass but for reasons of efficiency (Dugan and Stannard, 1985). The commission was innovative in economic analysis starting with its consideration of long-run incremental costs, introduced in Case 26426 in 1972 by William Baumol.

For the entire post-divestiture period through 1987, the New York commission was chaired by Paul Gioia, a Democrat and counsel to ex-Governor Carey, who appointed him in 1981. Gioia ran into several conflicts with Governor Cuomo, who took office in 1982, particularly over the question of whether ratepayers should bear responsibility for the costs of the Shoreham nuclear power plant.[3] The other Democratic commissioners for the bulk of the 1982–1987 period included Anne Mead, a lawyer first appointed in 1976; Rosemary Pooler, a lawyer and former Executive Director of the state Consumer Protection Board, appointed in 1981; and Gail Garfield Schwartz, a Ph.D. in urban planning appointed in 1985. The Republican commissioners, all of whom had been in office for at least ten years at the time of divestiture included Edward Larkin, a former state Senator first appointed in 1961; Carmel Carrington Marr, a lawyer first appointed in 1971; and Harold Jerry, a lawyer first appointed in 1973.[4]

How do the staffs of the two regulatory agencies compare? In 1984, the New Jersey Board of Public Utility had a staff of 323 people. The New York Public Service Commission had a staff of 641, or about twice as many as New Jersey. The size of the regulatory budget is a significant variable in the multivariate analysis. More important than size, however, in this comparison, is the composition and ethos of the staff. The New Jersey Board established a separate telecommunications staff during a 1983 change in staff organizational responsibilities from functional categories (e.g., accounting, rates and tariffs, etc.) to industry specialities (e.g., telecommunications, electricity, water). The new telecommunications group was headed by a lawyer, Heikki

Leesment, whose three deputies included two accountants and an engineer. The staff expanded from 3 to 40 employees in two years and was largely filled with young professionals recently out of college. No economists served in the telecommunications group and contact with the four economists in the Economic Analysis Section of the board was minimal.

In contrast, the New York Public Service Commission has had a separate communications staff for at least 20 years. In 1987, the telecommunications staff included 53 members, down from a one-time high of 90, because 37 staff members had been transferred to the Consumer Services unit to deal with complaints. The telecommunications staff was increased from 25 to 90 members during the 1970s, particularly following the New York Telephone service crisis of the early 1970s and the increase in rate cases caused by the high inflation in that decade. The AT&T divestiture itself did not cause a large change in staff size, as it did in New Jersey.

During the post-divestiture period, the New York telecommunications staff has been headed by Neil Swift, who has been with the commission since 1970. The staff is broken down into three units, a Tariff Group that analyzes costs and revenues, an Evaluation Group that considers technological and engineering issues, and a Planning Section that reviews capital plans and service standards. The members of the staff include accountants, engineers, and economists. The telecommunications staff receives frequent outside assistance from an Office of Accounting, a group of ten economists, and a legal division.

The New Jersey board has not received the same national reputation of the New York commission. Wall Street firms give the board a lower rating for regulatory climate in part because the tradition of New Jersey commissioners is somewhat more political than in New York, with many having served in the Assembly and later trying for elected office. New York commissioners have tended to stay in office for long periods or to go on to other nonelected positions, in government, business, or academia.[5] This difference in the politicization of regulation is not a trademark of all politics in the two states; in many areas, such as regional planning, New Jersey is a progressive beacon for the nation, while New York is constantly mired in upstate-downstate political battles on most significant issues.

Many observers support the relatively apolitical tradition in New York. An August 5, 1986, *New York Times* editorial criticized Governor Cuomo's dismissal of Paul Gioia and emphasized the need to maintain a relatively apolitical Public Service Commission:

> In the 70's and 80's [most state utility commissions were] pandering to short-term political pressure. But New York has a

very different tradition, thanks to the appointment policies of Governors Rockefeller, Wilson, and Carey, and the forbearance of the legislature. Commission chairmen from Joseph Swidler to Alfred Kahn to Charles Zielinski have been skilled technocrats, devoted to meeting state needs at minimum costs. They built a superb, nonpartisan staff and used quiet diplomacy with governors and legislative leaders to gain the appointment of qualified commissioners. (p. A29).

EXPLANATIONS

While I believe that factors within the regulatory bureaucracy explain why New Jersey made choices at variance with what the models predict, I must first review and eliminate possible interest group and contextual factors in more detail. Telecommunications regulation in these two states is largely the story of regulation of two companies. New Jersey Bell, which serves over 85 percent of access lines in the state, has long been considered one of the best managed and most technologically advanced local telephone operating companies in the nation. New York Telephone serves about 91 percent of access lines in New York State. New York Telephone experienced severe service problems in 1969–1970, and the firm has not maintained a good reputation among large users in New York City as a result.

The two regional holding companies have not used significantly different political regulatory strategies. Bell Atlantic has been aggressive about filing for rate changes and achieved significant success in moving towards efficient prices in Pennsylvania, Delaware, the District of Columbia, Maryland, and Virginia. In Pennsylvania, the Bell Atlantic subsidiary offered economic development funding to the state in return for regulatory changes. NYNEX also has been aggressive in pressing to change rate structures. Their New England Telephone subsidiary achieved significant local rate increases in Vermont and the "social-contract" (discussed more fully in Chapter 7), and received price changes in Massachusetts. If any difference can be found, it is that Bell Atlantic has achieved more regulatory change in several states besides New Jersey, while NYNEX has achieved somewhat less success outside New York.

The concentrations of large businesses in both states result in a greater likelihood of bypass than for the average state. In New Jersey, in 1984, the top ten business customers generated 18 percent ($114 million) of the total $616 million in business revenue paid by some 231,000 business customers. If ten business customers in New Jersey had completely bypassed the public network, $114 million in revenue would have been lost, representing about 5 percent of total 1984 New Jersey Bell revenues. The top 100 customers generated 38 percent of business revenues. In 1985, 1 percent of New York Telephone business customers generated 45 percent of all business message telephone revenues, 5 percent generated 71 percent and 9 percent generated 81 percent. The company claims that $67 million in revenues was lost to 119 bypass systems in the state by 1986.

New York City has the largest concentration of large users in the nation, particularly the Wall Street financial firms. The international dimension of business is also important; over 15 percent of all worldwide international telecommunications traffic either originates or terminates in Manhattan (Moss, 1986). Therefore, bypass is a bigger concern in New York than in New Jersey and perhaps even more so than the Fortune Service 450 headquarters variable measures. Furthermore, large business users have been very active in New York regulatory proceedings, more than before any other regulatory agency, except the Federal Communications Commission. The Corporate Committee of Telecommunications Users participates in all proceedings, representing all the major banks and financial firms, and the New York Clearing House of Banks also is a major player.

In New Jersey, large business interests do not participate actively in rate proceedings. The Fortune Service 450 multivariate measure for the bypass threat is the seventh-highest of the 49 cases studied, but it may overstate the threat because it does not reflect the relative lack of geographic concentrations of usage within New Jersey. A 1984 consulting report found that the bypass threat is somewhat less likely in New Jersey than in comparably sized states.

The concentration of large users in Manhattan, their political and economic development clout, and the regulators' fears of bypass partially have driven changes in telecommunications pricing in New York. Since the concentration is so extreme in New York, one is tempted to argue that regulators have had no choice but to change prices. Concentrated large users are not, however, the only major cause of policy differences in these states. First, although New Jersey has a lower spatial concentration of telephone traffic than New York, and fewer large users, it is still well above national averages, and this alone has not forced changes in rate structures. Second, Entman (1985) argues that several New York commissioners viewed the bypass threat as overstated and the administrative law judge who heard the generic bypass case agreed. Not all New Yorkers were or are terrified of bypass. Third, and most important, New York regulators had *already* changed prices prior to divestiture and the expansion of real options for bypass.

This third argument against the complete policy dominance of large users in New York verifies that the emphasis on marginal cost-based pricing nurtured under Kahn became an important part of New York regulators' decisions. Going back further, the large increase in the New York commission telecommunications staff that took place under Swidler after the service problems of 1969–1970, also led to an informed and innovative approach to telecommunications regulation.

Consumer representation does not differ greatly in the two states; if there is a difference, New York consumer groups are probably stronger. State-funded consumer groups have fought hard in both New York and New Jersey. Grass-roots consumer groups have been more active in New York, although they do not appear to have had a strong influence on policy. Grass-roots consumer advocacy is insignificant in the multivariate analysis.

Contextual factors do not seem to answer the puzzle. New Jersey has suffered extreme NECA losses, but that influence is measured well. The quantitative models show that NECA losses influence other states to change prices, but apparently not New Jersey.

Institutional factors are more likely to explain the puzzle. My interviews find that staff members think they have played a major role in decision-making in both New Jersey and New York. Top New Jersey staff members estimate that commissioners follow their recommendations 80 percent to 90 percent of the time, an estimate with which the commissioners themselves agree.

In New Jersey this staff input is the only major direct influence on commissioners. New Jersey Bell, the regulated firm, has extensive contacts with the board, but most of these contacts are filtered through the staff. Commissioners and staff both agree that the media, large users, and grass-roots consumer or public interest groups have played little active role in the regulatory process. Commissioners cite almost no input or pressure from the governor on telecommunications issues and only minimal input from legislators, always geared more to specific constituent service complaints than to general policy issues.

In New York, while staff input is also perceived to be influential, outside input and pressure have been far more pronounced. Large users in particular are organized, vocal, and actively press the bypass threat. The legislature is more involved than in New Jersey, mainly because of the need to change an existing law on real property taxation of telecommunications switches in order to retain large businesses in New York. Governor Cuomo has been involved, with the Consumer Protection Board, in negotiating the plan to refund 1986 Tax Reform Act reductions to consumers.

The emphases of the staffs themselves differ. In New York, Alfred Kahn's strong emphasis on economic efficiency influenced the public service commission staff to consider efficiency as a value in itself. In New Jersey, this is not true for any of the telecommunications staff members or commissioners. The absence of economists within the

New Jersey telecommunications unit and the lack of a relationship to the Economic Analysis Section helps shape this lack of emphasis. Some top staff members, when asked what they would do with a marginal increase in staff resources, mention economic analysis, but most emphasize more detailed, accounting-oriented analysis of embedded, book costs rather than studies of the relationship of price and economic costs.

The interviews in New Jersey present the impression of regulators and staff concentrating on minimizing the damage from deregulation and divestiture. Regulators and staff *react* to issues presented to them in rate cases. The board made all of its major policy decisions in the context of rate cases, some of which were stipulated by the major parties, and undertook no generic hearings at all. New Jersey regulators have talked about the possible need to raise local rates but have not implemented any policies leading in that direction.

In New York, the regulators seem to have several goals on their agenda. While protecting consumers is an important goal in the deregulatory transition, the commission also seeks the goals of economic development via innovative telecommunications services, telecommunications firms' productivity, economic efficiency and bypass avoidance, and targeted subsidies rather than broad cross-subsidies. Each of these issues has been the subject of a generic proceeding, in an active regulatory approach. This anticipatory regulatory activity has been "top-down," flowing from the commissioners to staff, particularly from Paul Gioia and Gail Garfield Schwartz. Again, this contrasts with New Jersey, where commissioners have not established a telecommunications agenda, but instead bemoan the fact that their staff does not provide them with more "bottom-up" policy options.

Both Gioia and Schwartz have stated publicly and unequivocally that they did not require or desire legislative assistance in implementing telephone deregulation. Schwartz, in a briefing to the New York Legislature in April 1987, insisted that regulators did not need legislative guidance in telecommunications, stating, "It is a popular shibboleth that regulation of telecommunications is in disarray. In New York this is not so."[6]

These comparative observations are supported by evidence from earlier interviews with New York regulators about telecommunications goals (Entman, 1985). Entman finds much variation across New York commissioners, but that "maintaining low local rates is not an overarching goal." Commissioners did not expect political pressure on the scale of that opposing the energy rate increases of the 1970s, and indeed, political pressure has not been so intense, in part because rate increases in local services have been offset by toll rate declines. Gioia has suggested that regulators have had an easier time with the politics

of telecommunications regulation because of its perceived importance to future economic development.

Thus, New Jersey regulators have pursued only one goal, low
local rates, and their staff has not pushed for them to do anything else.
Regulators do not believe that their pricing policies may lead to economic problems in the future. Regulators have been totally reactive
and the newly formed staff bureaucracy does not yet appear able to
develop policy options. In New York, regulators have pursued many
goals, anticipated problems, and handled them in an aggressive fashion, with help from an experienced, economics-oriented staff.

CONCLUSIONS

The degree of professionalism and economic expertise of regulators
and their staffs best explains the incorrect prediction for New Jersey
and the differences in policy between New Jersey and New York. The
New Jersey board has had no history of commissioner or staff interest
in efficient economic prices. The New York commission staff's interest
in efficiency was stimulated by Alfred Kahn and the reaction to the
service problems of the early 1970s. The New Jersey telecommunications staff was only established and expanded during the extreme turmoil surrounding divestiture; thus it is not surprising that bureaucratic expertise did not have a chance to develop to anywhere near
the extent in New York by 1987.

Commissioners and staff in New Jersey have talked about the
fear of bypass by large users but have not changed pricing policies. The
staff has been skeptical about the prevailing view of efficient economic
prices and has taken a safer reactive approach. The regulatory climate
measures reflect some of this difference between New Jersey and New
York, but perhaps New Jersey's regulatory climate should have been
rated even lower, at least for telecommunications choices.

Might New Jersey regulators just hold a stronger ideological
desire to protect residential consumers than those in New York? The
interviews reflect more of a singular concern with consumers in New
Jersey, but in New York regulators also have consumerist instincts and
they have had to overcome significant consumer opposition to price
changes. Governor Cuomo's commission chairman, Peter Bradford,
appointed in 1986, was known for his pro-consumer, antinuclear
views as public utility commission chair in Maine and on the federal
Nuclear Regulatory Commission. Still, neither Cuomo nor Bradford
has expressed any interest in further reducing local telephone rates
below the levels that seem locked in for several years as a result of the
moratorium and the 1986 federal Tax Reform Act. Low local rates

have not been the only, or perhaps even the main, goal of politicians and regulators in New York.

The differences in variables that are difficult to code between New York and New Jersey may have been important in other states as well. If data-gathering problems could be solved, some of these could be included in the quantitative models. The conflict level in New York has been very high; regulatory proceedings involve active participation of business interests and consumers of various types, leading to a rough equilibrium in interest group input. The New York staff is experienced in telecommunications and in complicated economic regulatory issues. In New Jersey the level of conflict has been lower, and the staff is relatively new to telecommunications issues. The professionalism of the commissioners themselves is another important variable that differs between the two states. New York State commissioners tend to come from appointed offices or academia, while New Jersey commissioners tend to be former state legislators who often run for other offices after serving on the board. Again, some of these factors are probably included in the regulatory climate assessments, but some are probably not included properly or fully.

Thus, the conclusion is that institutional factors not accounted for in the independent variable measures explain New Jersey's reluctance to change telecommunications pricing and competition policy. It would probably improve the quantitative models to analyze, measure, refine, and include such factors for all states, but that would require more time and resources than I have available.

7 Case Studies of Innovative States: Illinois, Virginia, and Vermont

The quantitative analysis in Chapter 5 has shown that institutional factors are important in state telecommunications policy choices. Predictions for innovative states that have changed their pricing or competition policies are most improved by including institutional factors in the model. In this chapter I analyze three especially innovative states in order to understand the processes by which innovation occurs within the institutional context of a state.

Some state regulators have made innovative choices that do not exactly match the dimensions of the two basic dependent variables of rate structures and intraLATA competition, particularly for the complicated rate structures of multiple services. For example, Vermont approved legislation that will fix local rates for several years in return for substantial freedom for New England Telephone in other services, which does not match exactly the pricing and competition dependent variable measures of changes made by the end of 1986. What prompted these state regulators to make such innovative policy choices?

Chapter 3 examined the range of potential options for state regulators, given network economics. For pricing decisions, proponents of economic efficiency suggest that commissioners reduce intrastate toll rates, raise local access rates, implement local measured service, deaverage access rates by locality, and treat business customers the same as residential consumers. Commissioners must also decide whether to initiate lifeline programs, whether to reduce the depreciation reserve deficiency, and whether to continue to subsidize rural areas by pooling intrastate toll revenues. For competition decisions, regulators face choices about allowing intraLATA competition, and, if so, under what conditions. These have been the major options available to regulators after 1984 and I discuss the mix of choices actually made in three innovative states: Illinois, Virginia, and Vermont.

Illinois regulators moved aggressively to eliminate all forms of cross-subsidies and to transfer access costs to end-users. Regulators in Virginia were the first to deregulate intrastate toll services and have stressed economic efficiency and deliberate deregulation. The Vermont legislature approved a form of "social-contract" that will not allow further large increases in local rates but that will allow the local telephone companies substantial freedom in the more competitive services.

The explanation of these policy choices illustrates legislative interaction with the regulatory agency. While state public utility commissions are structured to allow independent decision-making, telecommunications regulatory choices show political influence. How does legislative party control, shown in Chapter 5 to be an important institutional determinant of regulatory decisions, influence regulators? There is increasing interest in explaining the relative influence of legislative oversight and bureaucratic discretion in governmental decision-making (Arnold, 1979; Weingast and Moran, 1983; Schwartz and McCubbins, 1984). State telecommunications regulation provides a good laboratory for a test because of the abrupt federal policy change: "Because of the ambiguity in the surface appearance of the policy-making process, a better place to look for Congressional [or legislative] influence is in patterns or episodes of policy change" (Weingast, Moran, and Calvert, 1987, p. 516). The examples in this chapter illustrate cooperative relationships between legislatures and bureaucrats.

Table 7.1 shows the predictions of the multivariarate models and the actual policies implemented by each of the three states by the end of 1986. Table 7.2 shows the independent variables in the quantitative models in each state.

Table 7.1

Predicted and Actual Choices for Three Innovative States

| | PRICE | | COMPETITION | |
	Predicted	Actual	Predicted	Actual
Illinois	.61	1	.74	1
Virginia	.99	1	.05	0
Vermont	.28	0	.01	1

KEY: 1 = Changed prices.   1 = Allowed intraLATA competition
     0 = Did not change prices.   0 = Did not allow competition

Table 7.2

Independent Variables for Three Innovative States

	ILLINOIS	VIRGINIA	VERMONT
Interest Groups			
Fortune 450 HQs	28	14	1
Government Advocacy	0	1	1
Grass-roots Advocacy	1	1	1
U S West	No	No	No
CATV Penetration	35	45	47
Contextual Variables			
NECA Subsidies	-49	-38	13
Average Loop Costs	109	156	192
Institutional Variables			
Elected Comissioners	No	Yes	No
Regulatory Budget	15	23	2
Regulatory Climate	9	5	6
Legislative Party	Dem	Dem	Rep

ILLINOIS

After 1984, regulators in Illinois adopted efficient prices more rapidly and more completely than did any other state. Institutional factors seem to explain this policy better than interest group pressure or contextual factors. The Illinois Commerce Commission (ICC) has a tradition of progressive regulation and a concern for efficiency in pricing; the commission implemented local measured service for some telephone consumers in the 1930s.

The Illinois commission was the first in the nation to unbundle access from local usage (resulting in local measured service) and then to deaverage access rates across the state. The commission led the way in simplifying local rates by reducing 93 previous plans to two, residential and business, both of which reflected economic efficiency by implementing off-peak price reductions and volume discounts. The commission accelerated depreciation to eliminate the reserve deficiency, reduced the business access subsidy to residential consumers, allowed intraLATA competition in 1987 and intraexchange competition in 1989, phased out the intrastate pooling subsidy to rural companies, and deaveraged the toll rates of local operating companies in the state (Illinois Commerce Commission, 1987).

In its 1983 access charge docket, the commission began shifting the recovery of non-traffic-sensitive (NTS) access costs from toll prices to end-users in an effort to improve allocative efficiency and avert bypass. Regulators showed considerable concern about bypass since a Touche-Ross study found that 29 percent of the 110 largest business customers of Illinois Bell were already bypassing in 1983, with another 31 percent considering that option. The commissioners' five-year plan shifted all intrastate NTS costs to end-users by 1989. Illinois Bell, the largest local operating company in the state, serving mainly the Chicago area, is not included in the plan since their prices already cover most of their intrastate access costs. Illinois Bell, which has geographically deaveraged access rates ranging from $3.00 in Chicago to $6.00 in Springfield, had subsidized rural companies through a revenue pooling process that was phased down at 20 percent per year from 1984 to 1989. Consumers served by other local companies in the state experienced local access price increases up to a level of $6.77. As a result of this cost-shifting to end-users, intrastate access charges for long distance carriers were the lowest in the nation, leading to lower toll call rates in the state.

The Illinois commission started telephone deregulation prior to divestiture by negotiating with the U.S. Department of Justice to establish 29 Metropolitan Service Areas (MSAs) rather than LATAs in the state, to encourage competition and manage the many small independent companies serving the state outside of Chicago. As a result, Illinois is divided into more local calling areas than any other state, leading to more interMSA calling and larger competitive zones. As no other state took this approach, it shows that Illinois regulators were handling divestiture-related issues even before the actual breakup.

Regulators also initiated three major dockets prior to the 1984 divestiture that shaped their subsequent policies (Illinois Commerce Commission, 1987). The first, Docket 82-0292, allowed resale of telephone services in 1983 and initiated the competitive environment. Docket 83-0005 set up rules for the post-divestiture period and began to deal with the depreciation reserve deficiency. Docket 83-0142 set up the intrastate access charge policy.

Despite all of these changes, Illinois regulators have not deregulated themselves out a job; they continue to play an important role by ensuring the provision of quality telephone services. Illinois regulators have not simplified entry requirements significantly over those in place before the AT&T divestiture. The commission monitors closely local service quality, network performance, and billing. Companies must still file tarriffs for all local services. Local companies are allowed to develop their own rates based on cost studies, but they must price them at least as high as their estimated long-run marginal costs.

The commission quickly tried to show the advantages of the new environment to consumers. For example, when AT&T interLATA service was declared competitive, as the 1985 Universal Telephone Service Protection Act allowed (the name of which is itself a good exercise in consumer marketing), rates were cut 6.6 percent, showing an immediate benefit. Similarly, a double billing procedure for the transition to local measured service proved to consumers that most would gain from implementing this efficient pricing mechanism.

Why has the Illinois Commerce Commission been able to advance deregulation more than other state regulators? How have they been able to eliminate entrenched cross-subsidies? Although the quantitative analysis predicts correctly Illinois' pricing (.61 probability) and competition (.74) choices, some states have higher probability predictions. A full explanation of the extreme choices in Illinois clearly requires the examination of institutional variables since the multivariate model including only interest groups and contextural conditions (see Table 5.8) does not predict a positive decision on competition (.32).

Illinois' 1983 Sunset Law forced the legislature to become involved in telephone deregulation, since statutory authority for the original (1921) public utility regulation legislation (and subsequent amendments) would have ended in 1985. The result was the "Universal Telephone Service Protection Law of 1985," which itself expires in 1991. Compared to most other similar legislation across the country (there were at least 20 such laws by 1989), the legislative intent is quite clear. Case-by-case criteria are established for the commissioners to judge, but the burden of proof on telephone companies is small. Governor Thompson signed the law while noting that federal actions had forced Illinois to accommodate so the state would receive the benefits of competition. The governor allowed Philip O'Connor, the ICC Chairman, to publicize the positive elements of deregulation. O'Connor holds a Ph.D. in political science and had been Thompson's gubernatorial campaign manager.

The combination of a policy entrepreneur, O'Connor, and an economics-oriented staff, in a tradition of economic efficiency, allowed the commission to work with the legislative Sunset Act to make major changes. Although the previous chairman, Michael Kasten, generally had favored deregulation, O'Connor greatly accelerated the pace. He bypassed uncooperative commissioners and aligned himself with key staff members to push regulatory changes.[1] O'Connor became a national advocate of deregulation, emphasizing efficiency and competition in all public utility services, including electricity.

Economists were represented on the commission over the entire period after the Consent Decree, and they pushed the deregulatory agenda.[2] The commission economic expertise was "strong up the middle," like a baseball team, with the chairperson and his staff. The staff executive director at the time was a University of Chicago-trained economist with federal regulatory experience. The staff included several economists and policy analysts, who were not tentative in pushing their own agenda.

Interest groups affected Illinois policy but did not dominate decision-making. Potential consumer opposition to these policies was blunted by a preponderance of attention and resources given to a major nuclear power plant issue in the state. Rural interests were not able to halt deaveraging, as they did in most other states. The rural members of the legislature allowed the cross-subsidy to be phased out, in part because they were assuaged by a one-time 1983 AT&T refund that was distributed disproportionately to rural areas, and by the establishment of a high-cost fund for rural areas.

Illinois Bell aided the commission's efforts by not opposing competition, although many smaller, rural companies did oppose competition. The support from Illinois Bell was important because the company had a reputation as one of the best local telephone companies under the old AT&T structure; leadership in the company usually led to a high position in AT&T, with the last three AT&T chairmen having previously served as president of Illinois Bell.

Perhaps the most important contextual variables in Illinois are the high outflows of NECA subsidies and the low access loop costs. These both pushed and allowed Illinois to change prices, but alone were not sufficient, as the New Jersey example shows.

In Illinois an economics-minded commission, headed by a political entrepreneur, worked with the legislature to aggressively market the extreme deregulation of telecommunications. A strong cooperative company, Illinois Bell, and potential bypassers in Chicago, represented by 28 Fortune Service 450 headquarters, also played a significant role in supporting deregulation.

VIRGINIA

In 1984, Virginia regulators were the first in the nation to deregulate AT&T toll rates within the state. They authorized time-of-day price adjustments and other changes, but they did not allow geographic price deaveraging. Since then, the state Corporation Commission (VSCC) has deregulated telephone services substantially, though not so much as in Illinois. Institutional factors related to the professionalism of the regulatory agency and its close ties to the legislature best explain this deregulation.

Specifically, from 1984 through 1986, regulators initiated efficient price changes but did not allow intraLATA competition. This matches the predictions of the quantitative model, which predicted a .99 likelihood for a price change and a .05 likelihood for the competition decision. The Corporation Commission explicitly delayed intraLATA competition until the implementation of price changes, as recommended by its staff.

Regulators took a hands-on approach to telephone issues from the start. A Corporation Commission Task Force on telecommunications issues was formed in 1981, prior to the settlement of the AT&T case, within the staff Division of Economic Research. With the Consent Decree, the commission hired consultants to recommend how to handle the transition period. Meanwhile, a subcommittee of the General Legislature studied telephone regulatory issues beginning in the 1982-1983 session. All of this activity occurred prior to the actual January 1, 1984, divestiture. After divestiture, the commission took a professional approach to deregulation by establishing a plan for the future that relies upon generic proceedings to study major issues outside the pressure of rate cases and close staff monitoring of the early results of toll competition.

To recognize efficient economic pricing, the commission established an explicit local access charge in 1986, and regulators approved large local rate increases. The regulators seem to have accepted the new economic theory of contestability, saying, "We believe the threat of competition, is itself, a potent check on a firm's pricing policies" (Tuck-Jenkins and Milmore, 1986, p. 9).

As in Illinois, the Virginia public service law was antiquated, dating from 1900. The regulators needed the law to be updated simply to give them the legal authority to deregulate. In 1984 the legislature passed a law that specified how regulators should implement deregulation. This cooperation between legislators and regulators was enhanced by the ties developed in the direct election of regulators by members of the legislature.

The Virginia commission is the most powerful state regulatory body in the nation, regulating a wide scope of industries, including corporate charters, banking, and insurance, over which most other public utility commissions do not have authority (O'Toole and Montjoy, 1984). It also has a very large budget relative to the state population. The legislature traditionally emphasizes a highly professional approach to regulation. Commissioners serve six-year terms and are well paid: At $70,000 annually in 1985, Virginia regulators received the highest salary of any state regulators. Unlike regulators in many states, none of the three 1986 commissioners (all lawyers and all

Democrats) were professional politicians. The chair, and one commissioner who had previously been a staff member, served on the
commission since the early 1970s, and the third commissioner previously had held several legal positions in state government.

Thus, Virginia regulators took an early, active, and professional
approach to deregulation. The commissioners moved more slowly
than Illinois regulators in allowing competition but were dedicated to
economic efficiency. As in Illinois, regulators needed new statutory
authority from the legislature to deregulate. The close ties to the legislators, a large and well-qualified staff, and the professional approach
to regulation account for Virginia's extreme deregulatory policies
more than any interest group or contextual influences. The importance of these factors is confirmed in the quantitative model; without
institutional regulatory variables (see Table 5.5), Virginia is not predicted to change prices (.43), but in the model including all variables
(Table 5.3), it is strongly predicted to change prices (.99), as its regulators actually did.

VERMONT

The most prominent feature of telecommunications regulation in
Vermont has been former Public Service Board Chairperson Louise
McCarren's "Social Contract," unveiled in June 1985. McCarren convinced legislators of the benefits of the Social Contract and the bill was
passed in May 1987. Governor Kunin signed the law that allowed the
Vermont Public Advocate, a member of the Department of Public
Service, to negotiate with New England Telephone a five-year contract, subject to approval by the Public Service Board. The aggressive
policy entrepreneurship of McCarren seems a better explanation for
these changes than interest group pressure or contextual conditions.

Several provisions in the Social Contract benefit consumers.
These include stabilization of local rates, guaranteed minimum levels
of plant modernization, guaranteed minimum service quality standards, and nondiscriminatory access to long distance carriers. Other
provisions aid New England Telephone: relaxed rate-of-return regulations, relaxed prior notice regulations, relaxed toll price regulations, and immediately effective tariffs (in contrast to the previous
90-day waiting period). In its original form the Social Contract fixed
local rates at 1987 levels with no increase beyond a cost-of-living
factor. As enacted, the contract uses a more elaborate econometric
model based on projected telephone costs prepared by the Public
Advocate's Office. In 1987, the model projected three years with no
local increases followed by two years with an increase allowed up to 5

percent. The legislation also relaxed substantially the requirements for new entrants into any services. If competition develops, the Public Service Board can implement selective service-by-service deregulation or reduced regulation. The Social Contract replaces a 70-year-old regulatory definition by limiting regulation to interactive common carriers whose services are offered to the public, and it therefore does not try to prevent bypass.

Prior to the passage of this legislation, Vermont regulators raised local access prices closer to costs. The local flat rate rose from $11.00 per month to $18.00 per month in Burlington in less than three years, leading to extensive consumer support for stabilization. Regulators also instituted intraLATA toll volume discounts and expanded local measured service. Implemented on a trial basis in 1985, local measured service led to lower bills for 75 percent of customers, including gains for a majority of low-income and elderly consumers.

In February 1986 Vermont became the first single-LATA state to approve intraLATA competition for facilities-based carriers, and several competitors subsequently received approval for entry. The decision noted that local operating companies hold franchises but not exclusive franchises. Thus, while local competition is not precluded, no local competitors had emerged by 1989.

I find no evidence of important outside influences pushing the Vermont board to make such innovative regulatory changes. The policy entrepreneurship of Louise McCarren led directly to the legislation. No other state had adopted a Social Contract approach by 1989, despite the political appeal of keeping local rates stable while opening markets to competition (although the FCC's "price cap" concept, implemented in 1989, uses a similar idea). The quantitative model, which does not include a variable for such policy entrepreneurship, does not predict a positive competition choice for Vermont.

CONCLUSIONS

Innovative policy choices in these states are more a function of specific institutional factors, including policy entrepreneurship, staff professionalism, and economic orientation, than of interest group pressure or contextual conditions. In Illinois and Virginia, highly professional commissions made innovative and economically informed policy choices. In Vermont, policy entrepreneurship led to the innovative social-contract approach.

Political entrepreneurs, such as Philip O'Connor in Illinois and Louise McCarren in Vermont, lobbied for and succeeded in developing different, but still innovative, regulatory policies. Clearly, in each state other factors contributed to regulatory decision-making, but these individual efforts were necessary for policy development and implementation. The quantitative models, and particularly comparisons of the results of the full model and the "external model"—including only interest group and contextual variables—reinforce the importance of regulatory attitudes and thus, implicitly, this policy entrepreneurship.

Legislators have played an important role in each of these three states. Congressional scholars recently have analyzed the important oversight role of congressmen even when they might appear to be giving bureaucrats discretion and not monitoring them (Weingast and Moran, 1983; Schwartz and McCubbins, 1984). The significance of legislative party control in my multivariate econometric analysis supports the view that regulators are aware of legislative preferences, as measured by party control. These cases show that in several states, legislators have done more than simply review regulatory decisions; they have intervened and passed important bills. Legislative action was spurred by cooperation with regulators and the need to update and provide enabling legislation for deregulatory action.

State legislatures have not stepped in to protect residential consumers; no legislature has passed a bill to prohibit telecommunications deregulation explicitly. Conversely, no regulatory commission has moved so quickly that legislators felt a need to reverse them with legislation. Few regulators have been willing to take the political heat from small consumers that price changes bring, without at least implicit legislative support.

It seems impossible to understand the development of innovative policy in these states, by regulators and by legislators, without analyzing the institutional factors of regulatory structures and attitudes. No external interest groups were dominant enough in these three states to have achieved the policies that regulators are implementing.

8 Bypassing the Regulators: U S West

The case studies in this chapter show that even when an interest group is very powerful and it pursues an aggressive political strategy, institutional factors within the states are important in mediating the extent of the influence. Soon after the 1984 creation of U S West as one of the seven regional holding companies, or "Baby Bells," the firm pressed for deregulation to a far greater degree than its siblings, and has consistently taken a different approach. U S West's chairman Jack MacAllister said, "Divestiture created seven new companies. One of them isn't like all the others" (Vietor and Dyer, 1986, p. 151).

U S West has pushed for deregulation and competition at all levels of government. However, as the *Wall Street Journal* notes: "It is at the state level that U S West's deregulation campaign stands out for breadth and controversy." (Roberts, 1987, p. A-18). At the state level, U S West's initial regulatory strategy was clear; avoid public utility commissions and seek deregulation by state legislators.

U S WEST'S REGULATORY STRATEGY

In the 48 continental states and the District of Columbia, the seven RHCs average seven states each; U S West serves fourteen western states (not California or Nevada) with sparse populations and few large cities. The major reason U S West executives have planned a different regulatory strategy is the different environment in which they operate. Table 8.1 compares characteristics of U S West's regulatory environment with the national averages faced by the other six "Baby Bells," using the independent variables from the analysis in Chapter 5.

U S West states contain an average of only three Fortune Service 450 headquarters, compared to almost 12 in the other states; U S West is thus supported significantly less than other RHCs by large users in its efforts to reduce toll rates. On the opposite side of the spectrum, consumer advocacy in regulatory proceedings is less active in U S West states. Government-funded advocacy activity is rated "high" in only 28 percent of their states (4 of 14), compared to 60 percent of the other 35 states (21 of 35); grass-roots consumer advocacy activity is rated high in 43 percent of U S West states, compared to 57 percent of the

Table 8.1

Comparison of Average Values: 14 U S West States Versus 35 Non–U S West States

	U S WEST	OTHER STATES
Interest Groups		
*Fortune Service HQs	3 per state	11.6
Government-Funded Advocacy	28% high	60% high
Grass-roots Advocacy	43% high	57% high
**U S West	All	None
CATV Penetration	49%	46%
Contextual Variables		
NECA Subsidy (mill/st)	+ $19	- $7.5
Access Loop Costs	$ 27.8/month	$ 25.2
Institutional Variables		
Elected Commission	43%	23%
*Regulatory Budget	$5.1 mill./state	$9.6 mill
Regulatory Climate (1-9)	4.5	4.75
**Legislative Party	57% Rep., 21% Mix	66% Dem.

*difference significant at 95%.
**difference significant at 99%.

other states. U S West faces potential competition for local access from cable television; the penetration percentage of cable is slightly higher in U S West states compared to other states.

The contextual climate differs in U S West states compared to that in other states in 1984, although neither variable shows differences that are highly significant. The NECA interstate subsidies average +19 million for U S West states and are positive for all but Utah, while 25 of the other 35 states are sources of subsidies, for an average of –7.5 million for all 35 states. Average monthly local telephone access costs are about $2.50 higher in U S West states because of the lower population density and the consequent need for longer access loops.

While the external climate of interest groups and contextual variables differs somewhat for U S West in these 1984 figures, the institutional variables relating to the regulatory commissions and the legislatures in their fourteen states are quite different. Both houses of U S West state legislatures are much more often in the control of Republicans, some 57 percent while only 21 percent are controlled by Democrats. In contrast, in the other states, only 14 percent of state legislatures are completely controlled by Republicans, while 66 percent are controlled by Democrats. This difference is statistically significant at the highest levels; and we have seen that legislative party differences are important factors in both state and federal telecommunications choices.

The public utility commissions themselves show important differences. A large percentage of U S West states feature directly elected utility commissioners, 43 percent, generally considered, although not conclusively proven, to be more hostile to business interests; in the other states only 23 percent are elected and 77 percent are appointed to the office. The regulatory climate is somewhat lower in U S West states, 4.5, than in the other 35, where it averages 4.75. The regulatory commission staffs in U S West states are smaller and have budgets of about one-half the average in non-U S West states. This difference is significant at the 95 percent level.

We have seen that several of these variables, particularly the institutional ones, influence state choices across the country; therefore, U S West faces a different environment than its Baby Bell siblings. Contrary to popular belief, it is not high average access loop costs that differ most significantly for U S West; while the company operates in less dense states, most of the people and businesses it serves are located in metropolitan areas. The institutional differences are far more important: U S West faces a much more positive legislative climate for deregulation and a somewhat less favorable public utility commission climate. From a public choice perspective, U S West's strategy to deal with this environment in 1984 was totally rational.

The September 24, 1987, *Wall Street Journal* featured a front-page article on U S West and its high-pressure regulatory approach:

> Almost since its creation in January 1984, U S West has been arguing strongly for total deregulation of its prices and profits in the 14 Western states where it operates.... None [of the other six RHCs] is seeking deregulation on the scale that U S West wants. (Roberts, 1987)

The key element of U S West's initial strategy was to push legislators to pass bills favoring competition and a quick reduction in toll prices so that U S West could compete on a level playing field; U S West was willing to allow competitive entry into markets it dominated so that it would be allowed to compete more freely in lucrative new markets. U S West's general counsel, Larry DeMuth, stated bluntly: "Regulation is irrelevant in an environment of competition" (Vietor and Dyer, 1986, p. 147), and "The user is going to simply ignore regulation and develop around it" (Nadel, 1986, p.2).

U S West also attempted to move many of its activities outside of the purview of state regulators through the use of the holding company structure. Sharon Nelson, a state regulator from Washington, notes: "They create a shell under which to hide the pea" (Teske, 1987, p. 16). Ron Lehr, a Colorado regulator, provides a specific example: "Yellow pages were taken away unilaterally by U S West.... It was like the black ship sailing away flying a black pirate flag, while I'm rowing a dinghy of regulation" (Teske, 1987, p. 16).

In terms of legislation approved, this strategy worked well; of the 15 state legislative deregulatory bills passed in the U.S. from 1984 through the end of 1986, 9 passed in U S West states. U S West used it political clout and economic development promises to achieve this success. After 1986, however, due to bribery scandals and a political backlash against U S West's high-pressure tactics, the firm decided to tone down its rhetoric and become somewhat more cooperative with state regulators.

The three states discussed here illustrate U S West's initial strategy and show different patterns of success and failure depending on the institutional characteristics of the states themselves. Nebraska, Arizona, and Idaho have been among the most interesting states in telecommunications regulation. The Nebraska legislature approved a bill that has greatly decreased regulators' control over rates. Arizona voters rejected a referendum that would have forced further telephone deregulation. Idaho regulators fought to maintain the status quo and not institute deregulatory policies. In these states, U S West's strategy can be contrasted with regulation in Illinois, Virginia, and Vermont, each of which illustrates more cooperative and less confrontational interactions between the regulated firm, legislators, regulators, and consumers.

Table 8.2 shows the predictions of the multivariarate models and the actual policies implemented by those three states by the end of 1986. Table 8.3 shows the independent variables in the quantitative models in each state.

NEBRASKA

Politicians in Nebraska have adopted a different approach to telephone deregulation from all other states. In 1986, the governor signed a law to allow radical price deregulation of all services, including local service, the most extreme reduction in regulation in the nation. This radical approach is best explained by pressure from U S West and a receptive governor and legislature. Jack MacAllister, the chairman of U S West, called critics of such deregulation, "regulators who don't

Table 8.2

Predicted and Actual Choices for Three U S West States

	PRICE		COMPETITION	
	Predicted	Actual	Predicted	Actual
Nebraska	.13	0	.01	0
Arizona	.78	1	.01	0
Idaho	.31	0	.02	0

KEY: 1 = Changed prices.   1 = Allowed intraLATA competition.
      0 = Did not change prices.   0 = Did not allow competition.

want to walk away from their jobs" (Davis, 1986, p. A15). The legislation, written by U S West, allows local telephone companies to increase local prices up to 10 percent annually, with 90 days notice, unless 2 percent of affected consumers sign a petition opposing the increase, in which case regulators must hold hearings to make a determination. Services other than the local exchange are nearly free of any rate-of-return regulation.

Table 8.3

Independent Variables for Three U S West States

	NEBRASKA	ARIZONA	IDAHO
Interest Groups			
Fortune 450 HQs	4	7	1
Government Advocacy	0	0	0
Grass-roots Advocacy	0	1	1
U S West	Yes	Yes	Yes
CATV Penetration	53	39	49
Contextual Variables			
NECA Subsidies	8	64	13
Average Loop Costs	154	171	182
Institutional Variables			
Elected Comissioners	Yes	Yes	No
Regulatory Budget	2	9	3
Regulatory Climate	2	4	4
Legislative Party	Rep	Rep	Rep

The law retains some state regulatory control over telephone companies for a five-year period. The law continues strict regulation of local service quality and entry/exit. Despite the rhetoric about competition, the law actually protects U S West's monopoly by not allowing open entry into the local exchange market. The law did not authorize intraLATA toll competition until 1989 and interLATA rate deaveraging is prohibited until 1991. After 1992, however, telephone companies in Nebraska will be free to set all rates as the market will bear.

The legislature enacted the law despite the strong objections of the public service commissioners. Public Service Commission President Harold Simpson said, "How do you force good service if you don't have a handle on rates?" (Davis, 1986, p. A15). The state attorney general sued to have the law declared unconstitutional. In May 1987, a Lancaster County District Court ruled the law, Legislative Bill 835, "constitutional and valid." The opposition appealed the ruling to the State Supreme Court, but the law has been implemented in the meantime. Three Senate bills attempted to reverse the deregulatory legislation. LB 381 and 382 were defeated in the Transportation Committee. LB 380, still under consideration in 1989, would allow the regulators to determine what services are competitive and how to deregulate them.

U S West has used economic development levers to push for legislation to circumvent regulators who have been reluctant to implement large local access increases in the rural western states. At the time of divestiture, Nebraska regulators had a pro-consumer reputation and thus were an obvious choice for U S West to try to bypass. A 1983 investment analysis noted that "with the exception of Nebraska, the regulation confronting [U S West subsidiary] Northwestern Bell has been relatively supportive. While we do not expect the consumerism of Nebraska to spread, nor do we anticipate a full appreciation of the risks now facing the telecommunications industry" (Moody's Bond Survey, 1983, p. 3362).

While Nebraska regulators did not give Northwestern Bell everything it requested, after divestiture they were actually more generous than regulators in several neighboring states. In a 1984 rate case, Nebraska commissioners gave Northwestern Bell a $22.6 million increase, of which three-quarters went to local price hikes. Local flat rates rose from $11.64 to $14.13 in Omaha. In a study of rates in 17 western states, roughly corresponding to the U S West service area, residential local rates in Nebraska were only 12th highest in 1983 but were fourth highest by 1985, because Nebraska's rates rose more than in many neighboring states (Energy and Resource Consultants, Inc., 1986). Business local rates were increased substantially as well, with only New Mexico, among these western states, implementing larger business price increases from 1983 to 1985. By 1986, however, Nebraska regulators returned to a less generous policy. They chose not to approve any of a proposed rate hike, although by law their inaction on the case caused an automatic partial increase.

Prior to this legislation Nebraska regulators had not been innovative in their approach to telecommunications competition. The commissioners resisted intraLATA competition originally, but since the passage of LB 835, they have approved competitive petitions by MCI, US Sprint, and AT&T to provide intraLATA service.

Why did legislators pass such a radical bill, which regulators opposed, when the commission had not been totally opposed to gradual deregulation? Nebraska has the only unicameral, officially nonpartisan-elected legislature in the nation. As a result, U S West needed approval from only one legislative body, which may partially explain the passage of the bill. As in other states, U S West used its full political clout, including threats to shift jobs to other states, to get the bill passed. State senator John DeCamp was the main sponsor and advocate of the bill.[1] U S West used high-pressure tactics to pass the bill, including hiring a few legislators, who serve part-time in Nebraska, to work for their firm.

The bill also received vital support from former Democratic Governor Robert Kerrey who, as lead telecommunications spokesperson for the National Governors Association, sold the bill as markedly enhancing Nebraska's attractiveness to high-technology, telecommunications-dependent firms, as part of an economic development strategy. The state had been hit hard by agricultural failures, and almost any form of potential economic development seemed desirable. Nebraska did have a headstart in this area: The presence of the Strategic Air Command and several hotel chain reservation systems in the state showed success with telecommunications-dependent operations. This economic climate (although it was shared by many neighboring states), the unicameral legislature, and the support of the governor probably account for the bill's passage. As a success of the bill, Kerrey cited a telemarketing firm that established operations in Nebraska in 1986 to handle over one million calls for Kodak when it stopped producing its Instamatic camera. He claimed that 12 to 15 other firms moved to Nebraska as a result of the relaxed regulatory climate. Kerrey's replacement, Republican Governor Kay Orr, continued this general economic development strategy by offering telecommunications and data-processing firms substantial tax credits for creating jobs and expanding in Nebraska.

The following quotes illustrate former Governor Kerrey's position:

"You had U S West making the case for this all over its region, and here in Nebraska they had a receptive audience.... If they don't have to worry about some arbitrary commission of Nebraskans setting their prices, they'll come in here and show us what all their technology can do for our people.... If you live in a rural, isolated state like Nebraska, you absolutely need to be connected to the rest of the country. And there is technology coming along that can connect us much more closely. But to get it, we have to move away from arguing, "What should the price of the product be?" and into "What should the product be?" (Reid, 1986, p. A1).

An irony first noted by Gene Kimmelman of the Consumers Federation of America, is that Nebraska's "first mover" advantage protects the state. U S West wants to show other state legislators that this deregulatory concept will not cause political or economic harm, and therefore is not likely to implement rapid price increases in any telecommunications services in Nebraska (Roberts, 1986).

The aggressive push of U S West and the economic development agenda of the governors, as policy entrepreneurs, account for the success of legislative deregulation. The elected public service commissioners in Nebraska have not agreed or cooperated with legislative actions. Deregulation in Nebraska has thus involved minimal public service commission input, in contrast to the active role that appointed regulators played in Illinois, Virginia, and Vermont (see Chapter 7).

ARIZONA

A referendum in Arizona on November 4, 1986, Proposition 100, provided American voters with their first chance to make a direct statement about state-level deregulation of telephone service. Referendum instructions advised voters that a "yes" vote "would authorize the Corporation Commission to reduce regulation of some telecommunications services, and assure statewide availability and affordability of telephone services using definitions and procedures prescribed by legislation." Voting "no" would "require the Corporation Commission to continue to regulate all telephone and telegraph services" (Megdal, 1986). This extremely democratic approach to telecommunications deregulation policy was necessary because the Corporation Commission's (ACC) power was deliniated specifically in the state constitution, unlike most other states. Proposition 100 effectively would have passed the bulk of regulatory authority from the Corporation Commission to the legislature. This extreme form of deregulation was defeated by a 54 to 46 percent margin.

While several interest groups tried to sway voters, the competition was uneven. Mountain Bell, the U S West subsidiary, and AT&T spent $3 million, through a political action committee, to support Proposition 100. U S West was extremely interested in the referendum because, while Arizona totaled only 12 percent of its revenues, the state represented 38 percent of its recent growth (Megdal, 1986). U S West played political hardball in lobbying for deregulation and passage of the referendum. During the Arizona commission's consideration of Mountain Bell's 1986 rate increase request, for example, U S West threatened to move 1800 jobs to New Mexico if approval was not forthcoming.

Opponents of Proposition 100 spent approximately $50,000, and thus were outspent by about a 60:1 ratio (Megdal, 1986). The opponents were well organized, however, due in part to the efforts of the United Church of Christ, a consumer-advocate group active in telecommunications issues. They did not get assistance from all of their natural allies, however, because rural telephone companies and consumers were protected by a Universal Service Fund component in the referendum to maintain the cross-subsidy from urban to rural consumers.

The message that voters sent by defeating the referendum is not completely clear. Mountain Bell suggests that it shows "customers expressing confidence in the Corporation Commission's regulation of telecommunications services" (National Association of Regulatory Utility Commissioners *Bulletin*, 1986). A more plausible interpretation is that voters opposed further deregulation, as initial state and federal policies had hurt and confused them. Voters expected the regulators to move more slowly than the legislature because they viewed the regulators as captured less by U S West.

Prior to the referendum, the two legislative houses passed conflicting bills. The Arizona House passed a radical, Mountain Bell-sponsored bill to implement immediate deregulation, leaving only the local loop for Corporation Commission regulation—almost as extreme an approach as in Nebraska. The House bill was opposed by the state Residential Utility Consumer Office, the Communications Workers of America, the regulatory commission, and competitors, but legislators nevertheless approved it by a 2:1 margin. The Senate sought to achieve slower deregulation, with the commissioners as referees, although with legislative control as the dominant element. The Senate bill provided for service-by-service deregulation, a less radical approach. While commission interpretation of rules would have continued under the Senate bill, commissioners were no longer to be the main policymakers.

The Arizona commissioners are elected directly by voters and serve six-year terms. This provides more electoral independence from the legislature than in many states and helps to explain the conflict between the two institutions. Prior to the referendum, the commissioners moved toward economically efficient pricing more than did most state regulators: They increased local rates and reduced toll rates generally, as well as reducing rates on the four densest intrastate calling routes. The did not approve intraLATA competition.

The quantitative model in Chapter 5 predicts the probability of both these pricing (.74) and competition (.01) choices correctly. Using only the interest group and contextual variables, however, Arizona is not predicted to change prices (.46), so that choice is explained better by including institutional factors relating to the regulators, their staff, and the legislature. Arizona thus illustrates voter opposition to deregulation, despite the large expenditure by U S West. The legislature favored the U S West position but needed voter approval. The voters would not authorize increased legislative control over regulators in telecommunications despite the policies of the commissioners who had favored deregulation and efficient pricing more than those in most other western states.

IDAHO

In the immediate post-divestiture period, Idaho regulators were among the most outspoken opponents of FCC policies advocating a shift of costs from toll rates to end-users. The public utility commission tried, unsuccessfully, to order Mountain Bell, the U S West subsidary that serves almost three-quarters of the access lines in Idaho, to refund the 1985 $1.00 federal customer access line charge to residences that did not use toll services. Idaho regulators continued "value of service" pricing, in which households that can reach a larger number of other subscribers with a local call pay a higher local flat rate than those in smaller local exchange areas. "Value of service" pricing contradicts pricing at economic costs, which leads to lower access rates for subscribers in larger urban areas. Idaho's policies represented the most extreme opposition to telecommunications deregulation.

The commission explicitly set a goal of non-traffic-sensitive cost coverage at 50 percent local, 25 percent intrastate toll, and 25 percent interstate toll, and they ordered modest local rate increases towards this goal. Even when these goals are achieved, they will still represent a large cross-subsidy from toll to local access services. In 1984 and 1985 Mountain Bell rate cases regulators applied across-the-board rate increases at about 3 percent, rather than changing rate structures. As a result, from 1983 to 1985, average residential flat rates rose from $9.07 to only $11.31 per month, less than the national average increase.

Idaho regulators have been hostile to the notion of substantially increasing local access charges. They also have opposed other changes that would tend to raise local rates. As a result of their finding of past over-earnings, regulators instituted a rate freeze for Mountain Bell for 1987 and most of 1988. Idaho regulators rescinded their previous approval of accelerated depreciation rates, after the U.S. Supreme Court's 1986 *Louisiana* ruling reversed the trend of Federal Communications Commission preemption of state regulators and left states with discretion on this issue.

The commission did end intrastate access charge pooling in March 1987, which had helped subsidize local rates in rural areas. As a result, three rural companies filed rate increases of 200–400 percent, which increased the politicization of telecommunications regulation in Idaho. To protect rural companies, Idaho considered becoming a single LATA state, rather than maintaining two LATAs, and filed for such a change with Judge Harold Greene and the U.S. Department of Justice.

In 1987, U S West pushed the Idaho legislature to pass a deregulatory bill similar to bills it lobbied for successfully in 10 of the other 13 states in which it operates. Governor Andrus surprised most analysts by vetoing Idaho House Bill 149 in 1987, and his veto was sustained. Although the House State Affairs Committee changed the specific elements of the bill to which the governor objected, there was no time to reconsider the bill until the legislature came back into session in 1988. Andrus objected to a clause that removed commission authority over rate increases of less than $1.00 per month in a year and to removal of regulatory authority over customer billing complaints. The bill also forced local exchange rates that were below the rates in the largest exchanges to increase each year by one-third of the difference, to eliminate "value-of-service" pricing. Andrus said the bill "places the universal availability of the telephone in jeopardy for too many of our citizens." (Roberts, 1987, p. A18).

Thus, while the appointed Idaho regulators have made some minor changes in telephone regulation, the state has been near the extreme end of the 50 states in maintaining cross-subsidies and limiting competition. U S West attempted to use the same legislative strategy to compel deregulation that succeeded in nine other states it serves. A bill that was not so favorable to U S West passed the Idaho legislature and was signed by the governor in 1988.

CONCLUSIONS

Some observors characterize U S West's strategy in the first round of state telecommunications deregulation after 1984 as wild, extreme, and driven by ideology. According to Renz Jennings, an Arizona regulator: "U S West is pursuing a school-yard bully approach to deregulation." (Roberts, 1987, p. A1). These descriptions may be accurate, but they miss the political rationality of this approach, given relatively hostile regulators and far more favorable legislators.

While U S West went too far and ultimately lost political support in some states because of its high-pressure tactics, it generally succeeded in avoiding regulators and aggressively influencing legislators to pass bills forcing deregulation. This strategy worked partly because legislators have more incentives than regulators to care about economic development and jobs in their state. They cannot ignore the potential and highly-touted nonregulatory advantages of relaxed telecommunications rules, especially in a depressed commodities-based regional economy. U S West exploited this concern when it threatened to tie the economic development it controls, as the region's largest employer with 80,000 jobs, to regulatory outcomes.

Even when an interest group, like U S West, is very powerful in influencing regulatory decisions, the extent to which it succeeds is still partly a function of institutional factors, as the governors of Nebraska and Idaho, the three state legislatures, and the voters in Arizona, prove. The choices of regulators and legislators can differ; their domain of concern is different, they are accountable to somewhat different constituencies, and direct political clout can have different impacts. In the language of principal-agent models, regulatory bureaucracies are not perfect agents of the current state legislature. Their gubernatorial appointments or direct voter election in many states, their frequently non-legislatively authorized budgets, and deliberate insulation over time (Moe, 1989), make them far more independent than many other government bureaucrats. Models that ignore the importance of government institutions are not only wrongly specified but they will not be used by the interest groups, such as U S West, pressuring for favorable policies.

Thus, specific regulatory strategies of interest groups seem to be shaped by the political environment, although interest group pressure itself partially shapes the environment. While the latter situation may have been more dominant in the era of regulatory capture, the former may be more important in this era of deregulation, with multiple interest groups and entrenched institutional interests.

9 Conclusions

The causes of change in American regulatory policy, and especially deregulation, are the source of much debate. To what degree are changes stimulated by technology, interest group pressure, bureaucrats, or politicians? When and how can dispersed interests triumph over concentrated ones? Most scholars addressing these issues have relied upon evidence from a handful of cases at the federal level (Weingast and Moran, 1983; Moe, 1985; Derthick and Quirk, 1985; Knott and Hammond, 1988). A few have used the states as a laboratory to test theories of regulation (Gormley, 1983; Berry, 1984; Meier, 1988).

The evidence from the states confirms that both the institutional and interest group theories are necessary to develop a full explanation of telecommunications regulatory policies. Together, these two theories explain a substantial and significant amount of the differences in state telecommunications choices after the divestiture of AT&T. Incorporating variables from the institutional theory, emphasizing the regulatory commissions and legislators, helps explain state decisions to change price structures better than simply analyzing the interests of affected groups. Interest groups play a greater role in explaining decisions allowing competitive entry. Even for decisions about competitive entry, however, the quantitative model predicts state choices far better when institutional elements are included. It is particularly necessary to employ institutional factors to explain innovative states that have made substantial changes from the status quo.

This evidence supports institutional theories of regulatory policy, such as those of Wilson (1980), Derthick and Quirk (1985), Moe (1985), and Meier (1988) over the simple interest group theories of the Chicago School. I do not deny the importance of interest groups; indeed, they are an essential part of this analysis. Rather, when many interest groups participate and any policy choice holds significant economic or political benefits and costs, institutional analyses become essential.

The single-state studies, covering about one-sixth of the forty-nine cases, support the quantitative evidence on the importance of institutional structures and attitudes. They highlight the roles of policy entrepreneurship, staff professionalism, and economic orientation in making non-incremental change. When these factors are not present, as in New Jersey, regulators do not make substantial policy changes even when the interest group and contextual climates suggest that they would.

The case studies also illustrate the different types of interaction between regulators and legislators, particularly in innovative states. The cases show how one interest group, U S West, developed a strategy of bypassing a relatively hostile institution, public utility commissions in states served by its subsidiaries, to go to a more hospitable institution, the state legislatures. The next section reviews the specific findings for each theory.

THEORETICAL IMPLICATIONS

Interest Groups

In the deregulation of airlines and trucking, widespread consumer interests appear to have achieved a victory over more concentrated industry and labor interests. In telecommunications, however, deregulation leads to gains for concentrated interests and at least short-run losses for widespread, residential consumers. The incidence analysis in Chapter 4 clarified the incentives for different interest groups to attempt to influence regulatory policy. Large users stand to gain the most, rural consumers stand to lose the most, and a majority of small consumers face small losses from a change in price structure. The analysis shows that interest group participation in regulatory proceedings is driven largely by these economic impacts.

Of the interest group hypotheses, the expectations that the presence and political activity of large business users would encourage decisions to change prices and to allow competitive entry are confirmed. Their ability to bypass the network, to leave a state if favorable policies are not implemented, and their ease of organization give them strong political clout. Large users influence national telecommunications deregulation in important and underappreciated ways, and they have had a strong impact in some states.

I can not fully untangle the effect of large users from that of regulatory budgets in the full model for pricing decisions. Populous states tend to have more Fortune Service 450 headquarters and higher regulatory budgets, although these measures do not capture exactly the same concept, as the two-stage model shows. Large states are more likely to make price changes and to allow competitive entry because of the combination of more large users and higher regulatory budgets, *and* the increased pressure applied by long distance companies, such as AT&T, MCI and US Sprint, to serve the more populous markets.

The case studies enable examination of states in which large users participate actively and where regulators have taken their interests seriously. Large users clearly are important to regulators' choices in Illinois, New York, and, to a lesser extent, in Virginia. Politicians in Nebraska hope to attract large users to their state by favorable telecommunications regulatory policies. Large users, however, have not significantly influenced decisions in New Jersey, and innovative policy changes have been made in Vermont in the absence of a significant number of large users.

Recent economic theories emphasize the importance of large users of a service in stimulating deregulation. Their growing elasticity of demand increases the deadweight losses from regulatory inefficiency over time and puts pressure on regulators (Becker, 1983, 1985; Jarrell, 1984; Keeler, 1984). Jarrell, for example, argues that the growth of large institutional stock traders led to financial deregulation. My state telecommunications evidence partially supports these theories of the causes of deregulation, but finds that additional, institutional (or supply-side) factors are necessary, as well.

Organized consumer groups, including both grass-roots groups and those funded by government, have opposed price changes and favored competitive entry not directly linked to price changes. For the most part, they have not been effective in directly influencing regulators, although many state regulators (and U.S. congressmen) seem to fear residential consumers as a group when they consider pricing policies. The large negative intercept term in the quantitative model probably represents a baseline disinclination of regulators to change prices and incite the potential wrath of consumers, unless other factors outweigh this fear.

My consumer advocacy measures, from Gormley (1983), are not important or significant variables in the analysis, with the exception of government-funded advocates increasing the likelihood of policies allowing competitive entry. Gormley suggests that for regulatory issues high in complexity and high in conflict, like rate structure, consumer advocates have little impact, in part because government-funded advocates may represent conflicting constituencies. As the competition choices are less conflictual than the pricing choices, government-funded groups have had more influence.

Gormley's variables may not be the best measures of consumer advocacy, and are somewhat dated, although another study that tests Gormley's variables as well as other measures of state consumer advocacy finds little difference between them (Clingermayer, 1986). Still, I believe that more detailed and updated measures of the strength of consumer advocacy would have more impact. Even with better measures, government-funded advocates probably have more influence on decisions than grass-roots advocates because they have assured funding and do not need to arouse the public sentiment and support that grass-roots advocates require. The losses from changing telephone prices are probably insufficient to motivate consumers to overcome the barriers to sustained collective action. Where the barriers have been overcome, organized consumer groups do not appear to have made the issues salient enough for their constituency to influence the pricing decisions of state regulators directly.

The multivariate analyses confirm the anecdotal evidence that aggressive political tactics by U S West, in the 14 states served by its subsidiaries, have led to more deregulatory decisions. U S West subsidiaries are significant factors in encouraging competitive entry because of their positive attitude towards open telecommunications markets. The effect is very large: On average, states served by U S West subsidiaries are 96 percent more likely to allow competitive entry. U S West pressure also has influenced pricing policy, although no so much: Regulators in U S West states are 19 percent more likely to change prices than those in other states.

U S West "bypassed" regulators and went directly to legislatures for deregulation. This strategy generally worked well, backfiring in only a few states. To explain why it pursued this strategy, many analysts have pointed to the rural nature of the states served by U S West, and the consequent need for it to be aggressive in eliminating subsidies. My analysis of the 14 U S West states finds that institutional factors vary more than contextual factors, when compared to the other 35 cases. U S West states are different because they face more Republican-controlled legislatures, regulators with smaller budgets, more elected commissioners, and less favorable regulatory climates.

Cable television penetration is not a significant influence on regulatory decisions about pricing or competitive entry, although the effects are in the expected direction. It is still probably too early for cable companies to represent a significant threat to local telephone companies. Scholars and other analysts have discussed the possibility of such a battle for end-user access between cable companies and telephone companies, but cable firms have not yet become a strong factor in telephone issues, and thus regulators can continue to ignore them. In 1988, however, the FCC proposed to allow local telephone companies into cable television markets, which may raise the stakes in this potential competition for access to consumers in the 1990s.

Thus, the influence of interest groups varies according to their incentives and according to the particular policy choice. More interest groups are influential in state decisions about competitive entry than in pricing decisions because more groups favor competition not linked to price changes. Strong government-funded advocacy, for example, influences state decisions to allow competitive entry but not to change prices. Some interest groups, including large users and U S West, affect decisions about both pricing and competitive entry, but have greater influence over decisions to allow competitive entry.

Contextual Variables

Regulators do not appear to respond to contextual conditions so much as they do to interest groups. The only confirmed hypothesis about contextual factors is that regulators respond to the flow of interstate subsidies. Regulators from states that subsidize other states' consumers are more likely to change prices and reduce cross-subsidies in their own domains. Interstate subsidies do not influence decisions about competitive entry significantly, although the effect is in the expected direction.

Average access loop costs are not an influential or significant factor explaining state policy choices. This may be because loop costs have two offsetting effects. As hypothesized, regulators in states with high loop costs may be forced to change prices quickly because they require larger total increases to move to cost-based pricing. They may also be more wary of changing prices, however, because rural interests will be harmed if access prices are deaveraged. Similarly, states with lower loop costs do not need to change prices so much but as they are not forced to go so far by network economics, it is easier politically to do so.

External Forces

Overall, the combination of factors external to regulatory institutions, including both interest groups and contextual conditions, shows mixed results. Perhaps some of these variables could be operationalized better, but the proxies used appear to be measuring the theoretical concepts well. If the test of a good theory is prediction, the interest group and contextual theories do poorly. They predict state decisions only a little better than one could do by knowing the modal value of the pricing and competitive entry dependent variables and testing no model at all.

Institutional Factors

Having shown that state telecommunications regulatory decisions are not merely a function of interest group pressure and contextual variables, we must examine the evidence for institutional factors. Regulators, their staffs, and state legislators account for much of the variation in state policy decisions. The institutional explanation of regulatory change is much stronger than the interest group pressure explanation, especially for pricing decisions. The institutional variables, when added to the interest group and contextual factors, improve the predictions of state decisions tremendously; the institutional factors are required particularly to explain the decisions of innovative states.

The regulatory budget is the most potent explanatory variable and the most highly significant in price change decisions.[1] The importance of the budget confirms my expectation that larger staffs more fully analyze regulatory choices and find more reasons to change price structures than to maintain the status quo. State regulatory capacity is important. Regulatory budgets influence choices favoring competitive entry less strongly, which follows the normative evaluation of a less clear case for the positive value of competition in the short run. More analytic resources lead to more price changes but do not influence choices about competitive entry so strongly.

Furthermore, the case studies of Illinois, New York, and Virginia support the vital role of staff analysis in leading to policy changes. The importance of state regulatory staff is analogous to the role of the FCC staff in the late 1970s and early 1980s: "The Access Charge Plan reflected conversion of the FCC's professional staff to the principles of marginalism" (Vietor and Davidson, 1985, p. 12). This finding confirms that of other scholars of state regulation (Berry, 1984; Meier, 1988) and calls into question regulation in small states with very small regulatory staffs.

While the hypotheses are confirmed for budgets, the effect of the other regulatory structure variable is more complicated. Elected commissioners make significantly different choices about competitive entry than appointed ones, and different pricing choices as well. In both cases, however, the impacts are in the unexpected direction. These results suggest that elected commissioners favor the interests of the local operating companies more than appointed ones, and are not so sensitive to short-run consumer interests as is normally assumed.

Part of the reason scholars find conflicting results for this variable is that elected commissioners may have reasons to favor interests other than consumers. I have failed to clarify fully the complicated issues in the debate here.[2] Electoral support can come in many forms, not merely votes, and commissioners may seek it from businesses as well as consumers. Elected commissioners probably are more like legislators than appointed commissioners in the kinds of political support they need. State legislators have not been more likely to serve the short-term interests of consumers than have appointed regulators in state telecommunications regulation; in fact, legislators have been more likely to deregulate than have many regulators. Thus, elected commissioners may have acted more like legislators in telecommunications.

The hypothesis for the regulatory climate is confirmed in both of the one-stage models, showing that state telecommunications regulatory decisions are consistent with regulators' general policy attitudes and their decisions in other regulatory arenas. Better regulatory climates, as measured by Wall Street, lead to more innovative policy choices, particularly in pricing decisions, and in allowing competitive entry. This finding suggests that regulatory climate measures may capture the ideological predispositions of regulators, as constrained by their constituents, similar to ADA ratings for congressmen.

I was not able to treat regulatory climate as endogenous in the two-stage logit analysis because of lack of appropriate instrumental variables. The percentage of the state population that is metropolitan, the governor's party identification, the 1972 presidential vote, state median income, and average 1986 ADA scores for the state's U.S. Senators do not "predict" regulatory climates well. As Achen (1986) notes, sometimes it is nearly impossible to find appropriate instrumental variables.

While the regulatory climate can not be considered truly exogenous in a theoretical sense, it appears to be more a function of individual attitudes of regulators than it is related to other state demographic, economic, voter, gubernatorial, or legislative factors. There may be an unmeasured variable in state populations, which I call... 'the propensity to be concerned about long-run utility financial health, as opposed to short-run consumer interests,' that affects both regulatory climates and policy choices (through appointments or elections). As I cannot find other proxies for this variable, the regulatory climate is picking up its influence. The result that telecommunications choices correlate positively with independent (Wall Street) measures of regulatory climates remains interesting and important.

The case-study evidence supports the argument that regulatory tradition and policy entrepreneurship, two probable components of regulatory climate, have important effects on the initiation of change in states that have made innovative policy choices. These findings do not, however, answer the questions of how and why the particular regulators end up in office in a given state. That may be another project entirely. Over time, why is the regulatory climate consistently rated high by Wall Street in Illinois and New York, and low in Nebraska and Idaho? One possible explanation is history and tradition, as shown in the New York and Illinois case studies, that somehow influence the regulatory appointment choices of governors and legislators. Given that Walker's Index is related, if weakly, to telecommunications regulatory choices, factors causing state innovation in other areas are relevant in utility regulation as well. Thus, some factors relating to history, tradition, and political culture in states must be fairly stable over time.

Some political scientists use the concept of "political culture" to "explain" the residuals of a quantitative model. Wildavsky (1987, p. 5) has attempted to clarify political culture by defining it as "shared values in societal arrangements." Why such values should differ across states is not clear. Other possible, although not fully satisfactory, explanations of changes in organizational decision-making advanced by scholars include evolutionary chance (Kaufman, 1986) and political entrepreneurs who shape the political landscape (Wilson, 1980).

While searching for the best explanation of state decisions, I have considered several of the institutional variables that previous scholars find to be important in regulatory policy and those that I have expected to be influential based on participant observation. Other institutional variables could be tested. I have considered several other variables, including the number of commissioners in a state, the length of regulatory terms, the years commissioners actually stay in office, the average age of commissioners, and the party affiliations of commissioners. None of these are strongly related to the dependent variables, and including them in the regressions causes problems estimating the models because of the small sample size and multicollinearity. Furthermore, these are also likely to be endogenous variables requiring instrumental variables in a two-stage model. Since the institutional variables I actually analyze in the models, including the budget and regulatory climate, show important influences on regulatory decisions, I consider them the most relevant.

The confirmation of hypotheses about and the robust influence of legislative party control is important. Even with the regulatory climate and other factors controlled for in the regression, party differences affect policy in the expected direction. A change in legislative control of both houses from Democratic to Republican leads (on average) to a 41 percent increase in the likelihood of a price change decision and a 55 percent decrease in the likelihood of a choice favoring competitive entry.

State legislative party activity parallels that at the federal level. In 1984, for example, the Democratic House passed a bill preventing the FCC from implementing subscriber line access charges, while the Republican Senate considered but did not pass such a bill. Thus, while William Gormley and others suggest that legislators hold little incentive to intervene in these "zero-sum" regulatory battles, it is clear that regulators do take heed of legislative views at the state as well as federal level.

These findings add to a growing literature on the interaction of bureaucrats and legislators that has focused almost exclusively on federal policy decisions. State utility regulators are much more independent than most other bureaucrats, in terms of budgets, fixed terms, tradition, and judicial review. They generally prefer implicit legislative support but not legislative intervention. Gail Schwartz, a New York regulator, stresses: "Legislation should empower public utility commissions to exercise their discretion in every way, but should not order them to do anything specific." (Teske, 1987, p. 13). Lilo Shifter, a Maryland regulator, agrees:, "In this transition period, negotiation without legislative involvement is preferred." (Teske, 1987, p. 13). Nevertheless, regulatory decision-making is not totally independent of legislative preferences. The quantitative analyses presented in Chapter 5 show that the legislative influence on telecommunications regulation is substantial. It is especially important when legislators are faced with a strong advocate like U S West.

In the cases where state legislators actually have passed bills deregulating telecommunications, the bills are generally pro-competitive and likely to lead toward price changes. Most of them do not actually mandate price changes but leave the implementation to the regulatory commissioners. It seems that state legislators use telecommunications deregulation for credit-claiming purposes, leaving regulators stuck implementing the policies. State legislators care more than regulators about retaining and attracting jobs and industry in their state. Thus, the nonregulatory, potential advantages of deregulation—innovation, attraction of industry, moving their state into the information age—outweigh the largely "zero-sum" regulatory aspects for state legislators.

Furthermore, state legislators do not face many of the negative consequences of deregulation from consumers because the link between competition in telecommunications markets and price changes is not fully understood.[3] Thus, legislators probably find it unlikely that consumers can trace local price increases back to them, except in extreme and well-publicized cases such as Nebraska. Consumers are more likely to blame regulators for local increases because they make the immediately traceable decision (Arnold, forthcoming).

The explicit state legislative action seems to contrast sharply with U.S. congressional inaction in telecommunications policy. Congress did not pass any major telephone legislation in the turmoil of the 1970s and 1980s. As Congress has not acted explicitly, the direction of federal regulation has been unclear; the FCC has pushed aggressively for rapid deregulation, but Judge Greene has maintained deliberate control over crucial decisions in the aftermath of the AT&T divestiture. When Congress has done anything, as when the House voted to delay and reduce the implementation of customer access line charges in 1984, it has favored the interests of residential consumers. In contrast, state legislators have not acted to protect residential consumers but instead have favored industry interests—either the regulated company, large businesses users, or economic development generally.

Why have some state legislatures passed pro-competitive, deregulatory legislation when Congress has not? First, we must recall that only about one-third of all state legislatures have passed deregulatory telecommunications bills. Second, of the bills actually passed, a majority are in states served by U S West, whose pressure clearly has been the major factor. Third, in a few other states, bills have been required simply to update public utility enabling legislation that was 75 years old and that did not anticipate deregulation. Fourth, state regulators, as a group, have not deregulated so fast as the FCC. It seems logical that state regulators, the immediate and closest implementors of local rate increases, are far less inclined than FCC officials in Washington, D.C. to want to change prices. Thus, in the mid-1980s, Congress was able to agree implicitly with FCC policies, and influence them, as with access charge policy, but did not need to pass legislation. Legislators in most states, if they want to claim credit for any potential benefits from deregulation, must prod regulators to move more quickly.

Another explanation, focusing on congressional inaction, is that states generally have been forced to *react* to federal policies, including divestiture, Judge Greene's interpretations, and subsequent FCC policies. Although Idaho tried, states cannot turn back the clock, and must accommodate change forced on them. On the other hand, in the late 1970s and early 1980s, Congress could have tried to resist telecommunications changes. Congress faced more definitive decisions with clear winners and losers. In a sense, then, the greater authority of congressmen made their choices more difficult. Furthermore, congressional action is more visible to the public because of the media and interest group monitoring of recorded votes, which would tend to make them more accountable than state legislators. Some state legislatures have acted where Congress has not because state action only accommodates change forced upon them, and can not dictate fully national telecommunications policy, as Congress could have done.

Thus, state legislative influence, measured in the multivariate analysis as party control, is similar to congressional influence in favoring general policy directions. Legislators in 18 states passed bills from 1983 to 1988, but legislators in the other 30 states and D.C. had influence behind the scenes as well. Considered as a group, then, state legislators have not pursued a radically different approach from that of Congress.

POLICY IMPLICATIONS

The results of this study have important implications for regulatory policy. Individual regulators and their staff can have strong influences on policy decisions. Consequently, state politicians and activists should focus more of their attention on regulatory appointments and resources.[4] Nonpartisan nominating committees from which governors must choose, as instituted in Ohio and Florida, are good steps toward building a professional regulatory tradition. More resources could easily be raised by increasing the percentage of utility receipts for regulation, a policy that would improve analysis greatly at a very small cost when spread over thousands of customers. The benefits are likely to outweigh the costs, not only in improved analysis but in assuring consumers that their interests are being monitored and that telephone deregulation does not mean the complete elimination of regulation at the state level.

While I could not measure the potential influence of several other institutional variables, states may be able to use other changes to build a more professional progressive regulatory tradition. Salaries could be raised to attract the best candidates. An increase in commission size may be useful to encourage specialization in particular regulated industries.

These findings should give policy analysts reason for optimism, even if they sound like "good government" solutions. Regulatory structures and individual regulators are more amenable to explicit policy change than are interest group pressure or contextual conditions. Previous reforms in state regulatory procedures (see Scholz, 1982) made the interest group input process relatively open and fair. It would be shortsighted to improve the regulatory process, encourage more participation and the generation of much new information, and then not give regulatory agencies enough resources to analyze the increased volume of information. As Andrew Varley, Iowa regulator, notes: "Good information is in the best interests of all parties." (Teske, 1987, p. 18).

To amplify the normative conclusions of Chapter 3, I believe regulators should change price structures and then consider opening all markets to competitive entry. Regulators can monitor the results of these policies closely. The losses to small consumers will probably not be so large as many analysts suspect, and the worst losses to low-income and rural consumers can be mitigated by targeted subsidies in the name of universal service. The second-order benefits of efficiency and competition—avoidance of bypass, lower business prices generally, stimulated long distance usage, and, probably, more technical efficiency and options caused by competitive pressure—will be substantial. To lose these in the name of low local rates for all residential consumers, especially those easily able to afford higher rates, would be folly. Innovative experiments like "incentive regulation" in New York and "price caps" for AT&T are based on the possibility that improvements in technical efficiency may be very large and could even outweigh the gains in allocative efficiency from changing rate structures. Such experiments also should not be hindered by an exclusive focus on maintaining low local rates through regulatory inertia.

Still, the political costs of policies that raise local rates are high, as are the costs from attempting to introduce local measured service, a more benign policy for most consumers. Regulators must do better in selling the accompaning toll rate reductions, as they have in Illinois. They must also show that even with recent increases, inflation-adjusted local rates are still below those charged as recently as in the mid-1970s, and toll rates are much lower. Regulators must also address adequately consumer complaints about billing, maintenance, and service confusion.

It is probably too late for state regulators to shift the blame for deregulation back to the federal courts or the FCC, although some state legislators have been able to take credit for the positive aspects of deregulation while avoiding the blame. To survive, innovative state regulators must market the advantages of their policies. As Edward Burke, former chair of the Rhode Island public utility commission, says: "State regulators are sometimes too self-critical. Over the past five years, we have all dealt with one heck of a problem." (Teske, 1987, p. 11).

FUTURE

The American tradition of Madisonian federalism emphasizes the value of state policy experiments from which other states and the federal government can learn. Regulators have many policy networks from which to learn about telecommunications policy options. The main network is the National Association of Regulatory Utility Commissioners (NARUC). Other groups, such as the National Council of State Legislatures and the National Governors Association, hold conferences on telecommunications issues and try to share policy ideas.

By 1990 state and federal regulators have not gathered enough data to assess state experiments fully (but see Kahn, 1988). Only in the 1990s will policy changes show enough variance to allow useful analysis. Many small state regulatory staffs, however, may not be able to perform such analyses themselves.

It seems likely that states will coordinate regulation more on a regional basis, as adjoining states share regional holding companies that are increasingly active, and as small states can not perform much analysis. Regulators in New England and in states served by U S West are already cooperating. The cooperation in U S West states is necessitated by U S West's attempts to circumvent state regulation. In 1989, U S West eliminated its individual subsidiaries that had been operated by AT&T for decades, suggesting that some "Baby Bells" view themselves more as national and international telecommunications firms, than simply as holding structures for state-level firms.

State telecommunications policy may become more homogeneous in the 1990s as the benefits of competition and price changes become more apparent. It will certainly become more homogeneous if federal regulators preempt the states by imposing uniformity. On the other hand, the slowdown in local rate pressure in the late 1980s (combined with federal tax relief for the industry) presents an opportunity for state regulators to innovate without facing political constraints as tight as those of the mid-1980s.

Despite these changes and the momentum of deregulation, it is a safe bet that state regulation of telecommunications will not disappear in the near future. Too many complex issues remain. New technology, particularly the digital switches and fiber optic access loops that will be the backbone of Integrated Broadband Networks, may alter the economics of the network. Local competition is developing for large business customers, but may not develop in the residential market soon (it certainly will not if regulators keep local residential prices artificially low). Such changes, in turn, will affect the political environment, and state regulatory options. Similarly, international telecommunications issues are becoming increasingly important, as they both affect and are affected by state regulation. With so much at stake in the future development of an information-based economy in the United States, and with such a significant portion of the telecommunications industry regulated at the state level, state choices should be better informed than they are today. My analysis confirms that institutional factors affect telecommunications choices. Better policy can be made by improving regulatory institutions.

NOTES

Chapter 1: Telecommunications Regulatory History

1. AT&T argues correctly that allocation of "revenue requirement" is a more accurate term than "cost allocation." Costs are a function of network structure and technology, and cannot be allocated. Nevertheless, for ease of explication, "cost allocation" will be used.

2. The formula was SPF = .85 X SLU + 2 SLU X CSR. SPF (subscriber plant factor) is the proportion of local exchange costs assigned to the interstate jurisdiction. SLU (subscriber line usage) is the fraction of telephone usage minutes in the local area that are interstate. CSR (composite state rate) is the ratio of the nationwide, industrywide average interstate initial 3-minute charge at the study area average interstate length of haul to the nationwide, industrywide average total toll initial 3-minute state charge at the nationwide average length of haul for all toll traffic for the total telephone industry (Cornell and Noll, 1985).

3. Previous antitrust suits against AT&T had been settled, most recently with the 1956 Consent Decree, in which AT&T agreed to give away Bell Labs' research and development innovations rather than patenting them, in return for retaining its vertical integration.

4. See Derthick and Quirk, 1985, for details of this battle.

5. These rules have been challenged constantly by the RHCs. Some analysts argue that relaxing these rules would reunite local and long distance service within individual companies (Phillips, 1985). Judge Greene monitors the waiver requests by the RHCs and has been steadfast in upholding the three basic prohibitions.

6. LATAs were established through negotiations rather than strict formulas. Nine states have only a single LATA.

7. Equal access refers to "one plus dialing" for all carriers.

8. There was an estimated $26 billion in underdepreciated old telephone equipment in the United States in 1984, which, if recovered from ratepayers, would add a total $5.00 per month to all local loop prices from 1987 to 1992.

9. Centrex is a switching service for large customers that utilizes the BOC central office. PBXs are on-site switches that large customers purchase

to perform most of the same tasks. In 1984, the local telephone operating companies and state regulators were concerned that PBXs would make Centrex obsolete, but favorable pricing policies have protected Centrex.

Chapter 2: Political Economic Theories of Deregulation

1. Both the statists and those who believe they are not saying anything new (see Almond, 1988), should direct their attention to political support theories from economics that thoroughly ignore the state and its actors.

2. While some might argue that resources are endogenous, and that commissioners get the staff they want, there are counterarguments for an independent impact. Regulators tend to come and go (every 4.4 years according to Gormley, 1983), while staff members stay (10.3 years average). Budgets are largely fixed or grow gradually based on the level of utility gross receipts.

3. The statistics on average turnover in note 2, this chapter, suggest that staff members have a greater incentive than commissioners to keep regulating to maintain their professional positions.

4. Several states, including Ohio and Florida, have passed or considered legislation to "professionalize" commissioners in recent years, by requiring that gubernatorial appointments come from a list of qualified candidates prepared by an independent, nonpartisan committee.

5. In 1978, 74 percent of appointed regulators held bachelors degrees and 46 percent held graduate degrees; the numbers were 55 percent and 23 percent, respectively, for elected commissioners (Pelsoci, 1979). In recent years, more businessmen served on commissions, while economists hit their peak of 6 percent of state regulators in 1979 (Smith, 1984).

Chapter 3: Telecommunications Economics and State Regulatory Options

1. Any one access line is non-traffic-sensitive. The non-traffic-sensitivity of costs is not strictly accurate for users with more than one line, however, who must make decisions about acceptable call blockage probabilities based on their outgoing and incoming usage. This means access lines are intensively but not extensively non-traffic-sensitive (Wilson, 1983).

2. For example, high service standards are reflected in regulations requiring new lines to be connected within three days, and a Bell system norm of two loop pairs provided per each residence.

3. With existing technology, called SLC-96, electronic pair gain equipment is already in use for long access lines. Use of this equipment, which increases the number of conversations that can be carried simultaneously on a single line, will grow as digital capability expands.

4. Peak pricing theory dictates that peak usage should pay for the costs of that capacity required above the amount needed off-peak. Off-peak prices

should only reflect marginal switching costs caused by the call and not capacity costs. These switching costs are now very small and will decrease further as digital switches are installed. Telephone pricing has traditionally recognized these differences by offering lower rates at evening hours.

5. Economic profit, as opposed to accounting profit, refers to returns above a "normal rate-of-return." What is considered normal is defined by the risk of the investment compared to that in related industries.

6. Strictly speaking, marginal costs refer to a small change in service. As noted above, telephone plant is added in large chunks to achieve economies of scale. Long-run incremental costs (LRIC) have been used by the BOCs to estimate the change in costs from a "lumpy" increase in service. Short-run marginal costs would vary widely from customer to customer, and would be almost impossible to determine.

7. Some analysts argue that technical or "x-efficiency" may be more important in determining telecommunications prices than allocative efficiency. Under rate-of-return regulation, firms may not have incentives to reduce costs. In a competitive environment, or under an incentive regulation scheme, such as the "price caps" implemented by the FCC in 1989, they have such incentives.

8. See Johnson, 1982; Kahn, 1982, 1984; Noll, 1986; Ordover and Willig, 1983; Perl, 1985; Sharkey and Sibley, 1985; Taylor, 1986; Willig, 1979, and particularly Wenders, 1987 for a summary.

9. In the station-to-station view, access is also a common cost for other services.

10. Ironically, using technology to share access lines starts to mimic the "party lines" of the past, except that these are "smart party lines."

11. Furthermore, even if one agrees with the tenets of station-to-station pricing, and considers access costs as commonly shared costs, their proper economic recovery would be with Ramsey pricing, in which case local rates would bear the largest burden because of its demand inelasticity (Perl, 1985).

12. But Crew and Kleindorfer, 1986, show that with interdependent demand and low usage costs relative to access costs, Ramsey pricing can lead to access prices below marginal costs.

13. In 1984, interstate carrier access charges used to recover NTS costs added $.10 per minute of interstate long distance usage.

14. *Congressional Quarterly Weekly Report* 42, January 28, 1984, p. 129.

15. The companies tracked by the FCC represented 95 percent of U.S. telephones.

Chapter 4: Interest Group Formation

1. These categories are derived from Arnold (1979).

2. See, for example, the 1985 California public utility commission study that found average access costs to be $27.00 per month while prices were $8.25.

3. Other data reinforce the evidence for a relationship of price changes in this range. In a Bell Communications Research small business study, a $4.00 subscriber line charge resulted in a 30 percent drop in interstate toll rates, meaning over a 7 percent toll decrease per dollar of end-user charge. Actual AT&T experience resulted in a range of interstate toll decreases from 5.6 percent (the actual average interstate toll decrease resulting from the $1.00 federal line charge imposed in July 1985) and 8 percent (an extrapolation of the average 4.8 percent reduction for the $.60 federal line charge in July 1987), although these AT&T reductions were clouded somewhat by other elements. Other evidence is near the 6 percent interstate range. The National Exchange Carriers Association (NECA) calculated an average 3 percent cut for AT&T from the 1987 $.60 increase, which would mean 5 percent for $1.00.

4. Perl (1985) has suggested using this surplus gain to develop income-based access charges so that no demographic group would lose from reducing toll rates to cost and increasing access charges. This compensation strategy is in the Kaldorian tradition, by buying off the losers to allow the socially beneficial change to be made. Frequently in public policy issues, compensation is not discussed or paid and, as a result, beneficial changes are not made. Regulators could develop targeted lifeline programs to aid the low-income families for whom the access price increase would be burdensome, or income-based access charges that would allow all telephone subscribers to share in the efficiency gains.

5. "Before the breakup, a New York Times poll found that more than 80 percent of American telephone customers were happy with their service—according to the Commerce Department, that was the highest customer satisfaction rate of any business in the country", Steve Coll, *The Deal of the Century*, 1986, p. 367.

6. About 57 percent chose to pay $6.70 per month for access and $.02 per minute for peak usage and $.01 for off-peak. Another 24 percent chose $8.70 for access, $.02 per minute at peak and free off-peak. Sixteen percent chose the flat-rate option of $17.00 per month. The measured service options were capped at 35 percent above the $17.00 figure so that everyone could make the best deal for himself.

The politics of this particular issue continue, however, as a vote on November 4, 1986, in Maine banned mandatory local measured service by a 58 to 42 percent margin to "keep flat-rate local phone service at as low a cost as possible." Local measured service was not even an option in Maine in 1987. Consumers may oppose local measured service because of risk aversion; they do not want to face the possibility of a higher local bill in a particular month.

7. Access, local measured service, and toll charges are not the only cost changes to consider in a complete analysis. Directory assistance changes, buy or lease decisions about telephone instruments, and other changes affected total bills. For this analysis, I focus on access and toll prices since they represent the most significant change, but others must be noted in capturing consumer preferences about divestiture and deregulation.

8. Only 47 percent knew the name of their long-distance carrier. Some 73 percent knew that they could purchase their telephone instrument, but only 45 percent had done so even though it was very attractive economically. *National Association of Regulatory Utility Commissioners Bulletin*, No. 13-1986, March 31, 1986.

9. Analysts have not been able to generate complete residential incidence studies because few good data are available. AT&T has considered such information vital to marketing efforts and proprietary. Their main competitors, MCI and US Sprint, have sued to gain such information but they have not been successful.

10. The 1984 BLS Consumer Expenditure Survey interview survey asked 4457 households about their expenditures on a wide variety of items on a quarterly basis; the survey is used to develop weights for the consumer price index. I have used only the responses from urban consumers. The survey methodology is described more fully in Bureau of Labor Statistics, 1987.

11. The 1985 National Telecommunications and Information Administration report also estimated the U.S. average bill to be about $20.00 for interstate and intrastate toll calls.

12. The break-even points in this analysis are $25.00 in total monthly toll usage and about $11.00 in intrastate toll usage. It is likely (see Kahn, 1988) that telephone companies will not pass these percentage reductions through uniformly, but will give back more to businesses, through reduced weekday rates, than to residential users through evening and weekend cuts. Thus, real losses for residential consumers making most of their toll calls at night and on weekends could be greater, although these rate changes are subject to regulatory approval in many states.

13. If one assumes, as seems reasonable, that the median customer spent less on local options than the average customer, the median toll usage estimate would be higher than $11.00 and median losses from price changes would be reduced.

14. Thus, the median losses from intrastate price cuts only, versus intrastate and interstate cuts, are about the same. Intrastate prices can be cut by a larger percentage for a given end-user charge, but consumers make fewer such calls, balancing out to a similar net impact.

15. Bureau of Labor Statistics, 1987, pg.44.

16. This 2:1 relationship of toll expenditure from the above $50,000 income category to the below $10,000 category holds in two other studies (Congressional Budget Office, 1987 and California PUC, 1985). Despite the data problems and lack of regression controls, it may be a good estimate.

17. This relationship reveals about a $4 per month increase in toll expenditure per $10,000 income, the same as in the BLS data.

18. The $11,000 figure is used in this study, rather than $10,000, to link to the lifeline program in California.

19. Unfortunately for this analysis, the Bureau of Labor Statistics will not identify the states of interview respondents for confidentiality reasons.

20. On the interstate level, elimination of nationwide cross-subsidies helps those states that have been implicitly or explicitly subsidizing other states. In the explicit National Exchange Carriers Association (NECA) revenue pooling process set up by the Federal Communications Commission after divestiture, high growth states, such as California (+$175 million per year) and Florida (+$254 million per year), and rural states, such as Nevada and Vermont, have received subsidies from other states, especially from New Jersey (-$190 million per year) and Pennsylvania (-$116 million per year). This has been a national policy decision that is being slowly phased out. The implicit subsidies involve interstate services not priced at cost and the export of state taxes. These subsidies are also issues for the Federal Communications Commission, not state regulators.

21. In Iowa, for example, a state with only four Fortune Service 450 headquarters, business access loops are 25 percent less expensive than residential loops because businesses are located closer to central offices. Historically, it may be more accurate to say that central offices are located near businesses, which does not change the conclusion.

22. Some firms are willing to accept competition in exchange for price changes or flexibility, because in several services the threat of substantial competition is not so large a concern as the threat of access service bypass. The U S West holding company has been the most prominent example of this strategy, using a strong ideological argument in favor of competition. See Chapter 8.

Chapter 5: Quantitative Analysis of State Decisions

1. Logit assumes that the true regression model is "$y = Bx + u$," where we do not observe y directly but instead a dummy variable that takes on value 1 if $(Bx + u)$ is greater than 0 and 0 if $(Bx + u)$ is less than 0 (Maddala, 1977), and that the cumulative distribution of u is logistic. Another possible technique would be probit, but unless one has an extremely large sample, with many observations in the tails, the logistic and the cumulative normal distributions are very similar, and logit and probit yield similar results (Maddala, 1983, p. 22).

2. The number of cases in this analysis is 49 rather than 50. Hawaii and Alaska are excluded because their geographic isolation requires a different type of telephone network. The District of Columbia is included because it has its own public utility commission and a local telephone operating company devoted to Washington D.C.

3. Facilities-based competition is far more important than resale competition because in the former case competitors use their own equipment, while in the latter case resellers essentially act as brokers by leasing capacity and reselling it to others.

4. If legislative party control changed over the period, as it did in two states, the control during the more crucial period of telecommunications choices is used.

5. The auxiliary adjusted R-squared (AAR) column shows the results of regressing that independent variable on all others. Only the Fortune 450 and budget variables have high AARs, with the result that the Fortune 450 variable is insignificant in the regression and its effect is not in the expected direction. In this pricing regression run without the budget variable, the Fortune 450 variable is significant at the 95 percent level with a positive sign (see Table 5.5), but the regression as a whole is weaker. The Fortune 450 variable could have been left out of this equation with only small effects on the other variables.

6. The results also confirm that the negative sign on Fortune 450 in the full model is due to a multicollinearity problem, particularly the high correlation with the regulatory budget (.82), and that the impact of U S West is partially captured in the full model by Republican legislative control, with which it is relatively highly correlated (.46). The interesting interaction between U S West and state legislatures is explored more fully in Chapter 8.

7. State population and electricity generation are not highly related to decisions about pricing, which also makes them good instrumental variables.

8. The Fortune 450 headquarters variable is left out of this equation because of high collinearity with state populations and budgets. This variable could also have been left out of the Table 5.3 results with a minimal impact on the other coefficients and their significance level, as well as for the regression as a whole.

9. In two-stage models, the calculated standard errors must be corrected. In two-stage ordinary least squares regressions, they can be corrected fairly easily. In logit or probit specifications, the corrections are extraordinarily difficult (Achen, 1986). When I compare one-stage least squares regressions with two-stage least squares estimates, the endogenous budget coefficient changes only a slight amount, far less than the standard error of the coefficients in either stage.

10. When the budget is treated as endogenous in the two-stage analyses, it is as significant and still the most influential factor in choices about price structures.

11. Even though I am not able to find appropriate instrumental variables to test for the endogeneity of the regulatory climate, it is possible that some of the same unmeasured factors may influence both climates and telecommunications choices. If regulatory climate is partially a proxy for "political culture" that is otherwise unmeasurable, than its correlation with telecommunications choices is still an important finding.

12. Most analysts argue that by 1989 intraLATA competition, where allowed, is not thriving, except in a few specialized applications for large businesses. Some note other barriers to entry that state regulators have not or cannot reduce, such as lack of one-plus dialing and pre-subscription, while others predict that the economics of the network will never allow viable intraLATA competition.

Chapter 6: Comparative Case Study: New Jersey and New York

1. I worked as an intern with the Telecommunications staff of the New Jersey Board of Public Utilities in 1985 and with the New York City Office of Energy and Telecommunications in 1986, analyzing issues relating to the New York State Public Service Commission.

2. According to Dugan and Stannard (1985): "Chairman Swidler had been accustomed to fully distributed cost methodologies through a long and distinguished career, principally in the energy field. By contrast, Chairman Kahn was an active proponent of marginal cost pricing."

3. The May 1, 1987, p. A24 New York Times notes: "The breach between Mr. Cuomo and the P.S.C. has been the worst since Governor Roosevelt ousted William Prendergast as chairman in 1930."

4. Due to resignations and retirements, five new members were appointed to the commission in mid-1987. Dr. Eli Noam, of Columbia University's Business School Center for Telecommunications and Information Studies, is the appointee with the most expertise in telecommunications regulation and, as a political independent, is a good example of the professionalism of New York regulatory appointments.

5. Rosemary Pooler's 1986 Congressional race was an exception to that rule.

6. Gail Garfield Schwartz, "Managing the Mixed Bag of Telecommunications Services," New York State Legislative Briefing, April 29, 1987, pg. 3.

Chapter 7: Case Studies of Innovative States

1. This information comes from my discussion with Daniel Rosenblum, a former Illinois commissioner. This aggressive use of the chairperson's power led to its diminution in the 1985 utility law, balanced by the creation of a

strong staff executive director serving all seven commissioners rather than just the chairperson.

2. There were two economists on the commission, serving nonoverlapping terms over this period; the first is now a prominent federal energy regulator.

Chapter 8: Bypassing the Regulators: U S West

1. He was voted out of office in November 1986 (with 62 percent of the electorate voting for his opponent), at least in part due to the subsequent unpopularity of the telecommunications law he sponsored.

Chapter 9: Conclusions

1. When the regulatory budget is treated as endogenous in Chapter 5, it is still the strongest influence on pricing choices.

2. A better test would be a dynamic specification to determine whether elected commissioners are more likely to favor short-run consumer interests as their re-election date nears than earlier in their term.

3. State choices on price changes and competition are not fully linked, as Table 5.2 shows.

4. This conclusion must be modified by the reduction in impact from the regulatory budget when treated as endogenous and the inability to test the regulatory climate as an endogenous variable. The budget remains a highly influential variable, and it is influence per se that I am interested in, not the exact magnitude of the coefficient. Furthermore, the case study evidence supports conclusions about the impact of these and other similar institutional factors. I am not arguing that simply increasing resources and improving the regulatory climate will immediately change a state's policy choices, but these changes should have an influence on policy over time.

SELECTED BIBLIOGRAPHY

Achen, Christopher. 1986. *The Statistical Analysis of Quasi-Experiments.* Berkeley: University of California Press.

Ackerman, Bruce, and William Hassler. 1981. *Clean Coal/Dirty Air.* New Haven, Conn.: Yale University Press.

Almond, Gabriel. 1988. "The Return to the State," *American Political Science Review* Vol. 82, no. 3: pp. 853–874.

Anderson, Douglas. 1981. *Regulatory Politics and Electric Utilities.* Boston: Auburn House.

Arnold, R. Douglas. 1979. *Congress and the Bureaucracy: A Theory of Influence.* New Haven, Conn.: Yale University Press.

Arnold, R. Douglas. Forthcoming. *The Logic of Congressional Action.* New Haven, Conn.: Yale University Press.

Aronson, Jonathon and Peter Cowhey. 1988. *When Countries Talk: International Trade in Telecommunications Services.* Lexington, Mass.: American Enterprise Institute/Ballinger.

Bauer, R., Pool, I, and L. Dexter. 1963. *American Business and Public Policy: The Politics of Free Trade.* New York: Atherton Books.

Baumol, W. J., and D. F. Bradford. 1970. "Optimal Departures from Marginal Cost Pricing." *American Economic Review* 60: 265–283.

Baumol, William, Robert Willig, and John Panzar. 1982. *Contestable Markets and the Theory of Industry Structure.* San Diego, Calif.: Harcourt Brace Jovanovich.

Becker, Gary. 1983. "A Theory of Competition Among Pressure Groups for Political Influence." *Quarterly Journal of Economics* 96, no. 3: 371–400.

Becker, Gary. 1985. "Public Policies, Pressure Groups, and Dead Weight Costs." *Journal of Public Economics* 28: 329–47.

Bell Communications Research. 1984. "The Impact of End-user Charges on Small Business." (November).

Bernstein, Marver. 1955. *Regulating Business by Independent Commission.* Princeton, N.J.: Princeton University Press.

Berry, William. 1984. "An Alternative to the Capture Theory of Regulation: The Case of Public Utility Commissioners." *American Journal of Political Science* Vol. 28, no. 3: pp. 524–558.

Braeutigam, Ronald, and Bruce Owen. 1978. *The Regulation Game.* Cambridge, Mass.: Ballinger.

Brandon, Belinda, ed. 1981. *The Effect of the Demographics of Individual Households on Their Telephone Usage.* Cambridge, Mass.: Ballinger.

Brock, Gerald. 1981. *The Telecommunications Industry: The Dynamics of Market Structure.* Cambridge: Harvard University Press.

Bureau of Labor Statistics. 1987. "Summary of Consumer Expenditure Survey Methodology."

California PUC Policy and Planning Division. 1987. "Competition in Local Telecommunications: A Report to the Legislature." (May).

California PUC Telecommunications Strategy Group. 1985. "Charting A Sustainable Regulatory Course in Telecommunications." (October).

Clingermayer, James. 1986. "Government-Sponsored Consumer Advocacy and the Cost of Capital." Paper presented to the Southern Political Science Association, Atlanta, Georgia, November 6.

Coll, Steve. 1986. *The Deal of the Century: The Breakup of AT&T.* New York: Atheneum Books.

Congressional Budget Office. 1984. "The Changing Telephone Industry: Access Charges, Universal Service and Local Rates."

Congressional Budget Office. 1987. "Excise Tax Analysis."

Connecticut Department of Public Utility Control. 1986. "DPUC Investigation into Competition for Intrastate Interexchange Telecommunications Service." (December).

Cooper, Mark, and Gene Kimmelman. 1986. "Divestiture Plus Three: Still Crazy After All these Years." Consumer Federation of America. (December).

Coopers and Lybrand. 1987. "State Policy and the Telecommunications Economy in New York." Summary prepared for New York State in collaboration with the City of New York.

Copeland, Basil, and Alan Severn. 1985. "Price Theory and Telecommunications Regulation: A Dissenting View." *Yale Journal on Regulation* Vol. 3, no. 1: pp. 53-86.

Cornell, Nina W., and Roger G. Noll. 1985. "Local Telephone Prices and the Subsidy Question." Stanford University Working Paper.

Costello, K. W. 1984. "Electing Regulators: The Case of Public Utility Commissioners," *Yale Journal on Regulation,* Vol. 1: pp. 83-105.

Crandall, Robert. 1988. "Surprises from Telephone Deregulation and the AT&T Divestiture." *American Economic Review* Vol. 78, no. 2: pp. 323-327.

Crew, Michael, and Robert Dansby. 1983. "Cost-Benefit Analysis of Local Measured Service." Bell Labs Economic Discussion Paper #266, Murray Hill, N.J.

Crew, Michael, and Paul Kleindorfer, 1986. *The Economics of Public Utility Regulation.* Cambridge: M.I.T. Press.

Danner, Carl, 1986. Ph.D. diss. John F. Kennedy School of Government, Harvard University.

Davis, Bob. 1986. "Many States Deregulate Telephone Rates, Hurting Residential Users in Short Run." *Wall Street Journal.* 19 September: p. A15.

Derthick, Martha, and Paul Quirk. 1985. *The Politics of Deregulation.* Washington, D.C.: Brookings Institution.

Dixit, Avinash. 1980. "The Role of Investment in Entry-Deterrence." *The Economic Journal* 90, no. 357: 95-106.

Dugan, Dennis, and Richard Stannard. 1985. "Barriers to Marginal Cost Pricing in Regulated Telecommunications." *Public Utilities Fortnightly* (28 November): 43–49.

Dutton, William. 1987. "The Politics of Cable Television in Britain." Paper presented to American Political Science Association Annual Meeting in Chicago, September.

Economics and Technology, Inc. 1987. "White Paper on New York State Regulation." Part of Coopers & Lybrand report to New York State and New York City.

Energy and Resource Consultants, Inc. 1986. "Comparison of Basic Exchange Rates in Colorado to Rates in Sixteen Western States," authored by Daniel Violette and Lisa Chalstrom. Denver, Colorado.

Entman, Robert, 1985. "Issues in Telecommunications Regulation and Competition: Early Policy Perspectives from the States." Center for Information Policy Research: Harvard University.

Ferejohn, John, 1974. *Pork Barrel Politics*. Palo Alto, Calif.: Stanford University Press.

General Accounting Office Report. 1986. "Telephone Communications: Bypass of the Local Telephone Companies." Washington, D.C.

Gormley, William. 1983. *The Politics of Public Utility Regulation*. Pittsburgh, Pa.: University of Pittsburgh Press.

Gujarati, Damodar. 1978. *Basic Econometrics*. New York: McGraw Hill.

Harris, Malcolm, and Peter Navarro. 1983. "Does Electing Commissioners Bring Lower Electricity Rates?" *Public Utilities Fortnightly* (1 September): 23–27.

Harris, Robert. 1988. "Telecommunications Policy in Japan: Lessons for the U.S.," paper presented to the Sixteenth Annual Telecommunications Policy Research Conference, Airlie, Virginia, October.

Hendricks, Wallace. 1989. Comments made at "Divestiture: Five Years Later." Conference held March 2–3 in Washington, D.C., sponsored by Columbia University's Center for Telecommunications and Information Studies.

Horwitz, Robert, 1989. *The Irony of Regulatory Reform*. New York: Oxford Press.

Huntington, Samuel. 1952. "The Marasmus of the ICC." *Yale Law Journal* 6: 467–509.

Illinois Commerce Commission Policy Analysis Staff Monograph. 1987.

Irwin, Manley. 1984. *Telecommunications America: Markets Without Boundaries*. Westport, Conn.: Quorum Books.

Jarrell, Greg. 1984. "Change at the Exchange: The Causes and Effects of Deregulation." *Journal of Law and Economics* (October): Vol 27, no. 2: 273–312.

Johnson, Leland L. 1982. "Competition and Cross-Subsidization in the Telephone Industry." Rand Corporation Publication, Santa Monica, California.

Johnson, Leland, and Rolla Edward Park. 1986. "LMS Analysis." Rand Corporation, Santa Monica, California.

Joskow, Paul. 1972. "The Determination of the Allowed Rate of Return in a Formal Regulatory Hearing." *Bell Journal of Economics and Management Science* 3: 632-44.

Joskow, Paul. 1973. "Pricing Decisions of Regulated Firms: A Behavioral Approach." *Bell Journal of Economics and Management Science* 4: 118-40.

Joskow, Paul. 1974. "Inflation and Environmental Concern." *Journal of Law and Economics* (October): 291-328.

Joskow, Paul L., and Roger G. Noll. 1981. "Regulation in Theory and Practice: An Overview." In *Studies in Public Regulation*, edited by Gary Fromm, pp. 1-65. Cambridge: M.I.T. Press.

Kahaner, Larry. 1987. *On The Line: The Men of MCI Who Took on AT&T, Risked Everything and Won.* New York: Warner Books.

Kahn, Alfred E. 1982. "Some Thoughts on Telephone Access Pricing." Delivered at Workshop on Local Access: Strategies for Public Policy, St. Louis, Mo., September.

Kahn, Alfred E. 1984. "The Next Steps in Telecommunications Regulation and Research." *Public Utilities Fortnightly* (19 July): 13-18.

Kahn, Brenda. 1988. "Price Cap vs. Cost of Service Regulation: Evidence from Intrastate Toll Pricing." Paper delivered to Rutgers University Conference on Public Utility Regulation, Monterey, California, July 6-8.

Kalt, Joseph. 1981. *The Economics and Politics of Oil Price Regulation.* Cambridge: M.I.T. Press.

Kalt, Joseph, and Mark Zupan. 1984. "Capture versus Ideology in the Economic Theory of Politics," *American Economic Review* 74 (July): 279-300.

Katzman, Robert. 1980. *Regulatory Bureaucracy.* Cambridge: M.I.T. Press.

Kaufman, Herbert. 1986. *Time, Chance, and Organizations: Natural Selection in A Perilous Environment.* Chatham, N.J.: Chatham House.

Keeler, Theodore. 1984. "Theories of regulation and the deregulation movement." *Public Choice.* Vol. 44: pp. 103-146.

Kennedy, Peter. 1985. *A Guide to Econometrics.* Cambridge: M.I.T. Press.

Kingdon, John. 1988. "Ideas, Politics and Public Policies," paper presented to the Annual Meeting of the American Political Science Association, Washington, D.C., September.

Kirkland, Richard, 1984. "Ma Blue: IBM's Move Into Communications," in *Fortune* magazine, pp. 52-56, October 15.

Kmenta, Jan. 1986. *Elements of Econometrics.* New York: Macmillan.

Knott, Jack, and Thomas Hammond. 1988. "The Deregulatory Snowball: Explaining Deregulation in the Financial Industry." *Journal of Politics* (February): 3-30.

Konrad, Fred. 1985. "At the Forefront of Evolvement to a Fully Competitive Telephone Marketplace." *Public Utilities Fortnightly* (3 October): 48-51.

Kraemer, Joseph. 1985. "An Analysis of Local Exchange Bypass." In *The Impact of Deregulation and Market Forces on Public Utilities*, edited by Patrick Mann and Harry Trebing, pp. 59-64, East Lansing, Michigan, Michigan State University.

Leone, Robert. 1986. *Who Profits? Winners, Losers, and Government Regulation.* New York: Basic Books.

Leone, Robert and John Jackson. 1981. "The Political Economy of Federal Regulatory Activity: The Case of Water Pollution Controls," Chap. 5 in *Studies in Public Regulation,* edited by Gary Fromm. Cambridge: M.I.T. Press.

Levine, Michael. 1981. "Revisionism Revised: Airline Deregulation and the Public Interest." *Law and Contemporary Problems* 44: 179-195.

Lindblom, Charles. 1977. *Politics and Markets.* New York: Basic Books.

Long, Norton. 1958. "The Local Community as an Ecology of Games," *American Journal of Sociology* 64: 251-61.

Lowi, Theodore J. 1969. *The End of Liberalism.* New York: W. W. Norton.

MacAvoy, Paul and Kenneth Robinson. 1983. "Winning By Losing: The AT&T Settlement and Its Impact on Telecommunications." *Yale Journal on Regulation* 1, no. 1: 1-42.

Maddala, G. S. 1977. *Econometrics.* New York: McGraw Hill.

Maddala, G.S. 1983. *Limited Dependent and Qualitative Variables in Econometrics.* New York: Cambridge University Press.

Maher, William F., Jr. 1985. "Legal Aspects of State and Federal Regulatory Jurisdiction Over the Telephone Industry: A Survey." Center for Information Policy Research Monograph: Harvard University.

Mann, Patrick, and Walter Primeaux. 1983. "The Controversial Question of Commissioner Selection." *Public Utilities Fortnightly* (17 March): 21-24.

McCraw, Thomas K. 1984. *Prophets of Regulation.* Cambridge: Harvard University Press.

Megdal, Sharon Bernstein. 1986. "The Political Economy of Telecommunications Deregulation in Arizona." Paper presented to the Forum on Telecommunications Deregulation, Tucson, Arizona. June 5-6.

Meier, Kenneth. 1985. *Regulation: Politics, Bureaucracy, and Economics.* New York: St. Martin's Press.

Meier, Kenneth. 1988. *The Political Economy of Regulation: The Case of Insurance.* Albany: State University of New York Press.

Meyer, John, Robert Wilson, Alan Baughcum, Ellen Burton, and Louis Caouette. 1980. *The Economics of Competition in the Telecommunications Industry.* Cambridge, Mass.: Oelgeschlager, Gunn and Hain.

Miles, Robert, and Vinrod Bhambri. 1983. *The Regulatory Executives.* Beverly Hills Ca.: Sage Publications.

Mitnick, Barry. 1980. *The Political Economy of Regulation: Creating, Designing and Removing Regulatory Forms.* New York: Columbia University Press.

Moe, Terry. 1982. "Regulatory Performance and Presidential Administration." *American Journal of Political Science.* 26 (May): 197-224.

Moe, Terry. 1985. "Control and Feedback in Economic Regulation: The Case of the NLRB." *American Political Science Review.* 79 (December): 1094-1116.

Moe, Terry. 1989. "The Politics of Bureaucratic Structure." In *Can the Government Govern?* edited by John Chubb and Paul Peterson, pp. 267-329. Washington, D.C.: Brookings Institution.

Moody's Bond Survey. 1983. "Special Report on the AT&T Divestiture." Vol. 75, no. 11, New York.

Moss, Mitchell. 1986. "Can States Face the Future? A New Agenda for Telecommunications Policy." *New York Affairs,* Vol 9, no. 3: pp. 81-93.

Nadel, Mark. 1986. "The Changing Mission of Telecommunications Regulators At the State Level." Aspen Institute Conference, August 26-30. Aspen, Colorado.

Nagel, Jack. 1975. *The Descriptive Analysis of Power.* New Haven, Conn.: Yale University Press.

National Association of Regulatory Utility Commissioners. 1984-1987. *Bulletin.*

National Telecommunications and Information Administration. 1985. "Competition Benefits Report." U.S. Department of Commerce.

National Telecommunications and Information Administration Office of Policy Analysis and Development. 1986. "Telephone Competition and Deregulation: A Survey of the States." Washington, D.C. NTIA Report 86-205.

Navarro, Peter. 1985. *The Dimming of America: The Real Costs of Electric Utility Regulatory Failure.* Cambridge, Mass.: Ballinger.

Niskanen, William, 1971. *Bureaucracy and Representative Government.* Chicago: Aldine.

Noam, Eli. 1983. "Federal and State Roles in Telecommunications: The Effects of Deregulation." Research Working Paper, Columbia University Center for Telecommunications and Information Studies.

Noll, Roger. 1986. "State Regulatory Responses to Competition and Divestiture in the Telecommunications Industry." in *Antitrust and Regulation,* edited by Ronald Grieson, pp. 165-200. Lexington, Mass.: D.C. Heath.

Nordlinger, Eric. 1981. *On the Autonomy of the Democratic State.* Cambridge: Harvard University Press.

Olson, Mancur. 1965. *The Logic of Collective Action.* Cambridge: Harvard University Press.

Ordover, Janusz, and Robert Willig. 1983. "Local Telephone Pricing in a Competitive Environment." In *Telecommunications Regulation Today and Tomorrow,* edited by Eli Noam, pp. 267-290. New York: Harcourt Brace Jovanovich.

O'Toole, Laurence, and Robert Montjoy. 1984. *Regulatory Decision Making: The Virginia State Corporation Commission.* Charlottesville: University of Virginia Press.

Pelsoci, Thomas. 1979. "Organizational Correlates of Utility Rates." In *Energy and Environmental Issues,* edited by Michael Steinman, pp. 101-116. Lexington, Mass.: D. C. Heath.

Peltzman, Sam. 1976. "Toward A More General Theory of Regulation." *Journal of Law and Economics* 19: 211-240.

Perl, Lewis J. 1983. "Residential Demand for Telephone Service." National Economic Research Associates. White Plains, New York.

Perl, Lewis J. 1985. "Social Welfare and Distributional Consequences of Cost-Based Telephone Pricing." National Economic Research Associates. White Plains, New York.

Phillips, Almarin. 1982. "On the Impossibility of Competition in Telecommunications: Public Policy Gone Awry." In *Regulatory Reform and Public Utilities*, edited by Michael Crew, pp. 7-34, Lexington, Mass.: D. C. Heath.

Phillips, Almarin. 1985. "The Reintegration of Telecommunications: An Interim View." In *Analyzing the Impact of Regulatory Change in Public Utilities*, edited by Michael Crew, pp. 5-16, Lexington, Mass.: D. C. Heath.

Posner, Richard A. 1971. "Taxation by Regulation." *Bell Journal of Economics and Management Science* 2: 548-643.

Posner, Richard A. 1974. "Theories of Economic Regulation." *Bell Journal of Economics and Management Science* 5 (Autumn): 337-52.

Quirk, Paul. 1981. *Industry Influence in Federal Regulatory Agencies*. Princeton, N.J.: Princeton University Press.

Quirk, Paul. 1988. "Ideas, Interests, and Deregulation: The Politics of Ideas in Congress," paper presented to the Annual Meeting of the American Political Science Association, Washington, D.C., September.

Ramsey, Frank. 1927. "A Contribution to the Theory of Taxation." *Economic Journal* (March): 47-61.

Reid, T. R. 1986. "Phone Deregulation, Phase 2." *Washington Post*, 27 May: A-1.

Roberts, Johnnie. 1986. "Nebraska Law Deregulating Phone Rates May Spur Some Changes in Other States." *Wall Street Journal*, 5 May: 14.

Roberts, Johnnie. 1987. "U S West, Demanding Future Deregulation, Sparks Much Criticism." *Wall Street Journal* 24 September: A-1.

Rohlfs, Jeffrey. 1979. "Economically Efficient Bell System Pricing." Bell Labs Economic Discussion Paper #138, Murray Hill, N.J.

Rudd, David O. 1985. "The Illinois Universal Telephone Service Protection Law of 1985: A Path to Competition." Illinois Commerce Commission Staff Monograph. Chicago, Illinois.

Schwartz, Thomas, and Mathew McCubbins. 1984. "Congressional Oversight Overlooked: Fire Alarms and Police Patrols." *American Journal of Political Science*. Vol 2, no. 1: pp. 165-179.

Scholz, John. 1982. "State Regulatory Reform." *Policy Studies Review*, Vol. 1, no. 2: pp. 347-360.

Sharkey, William. 1983. "Outline of a Positive Theory of Regulation." In *Proceedings from the Tenth Annual Telecommunications Policy Research Conference*, edited by Oscar Gandy, Paul Espinosa, and Janusz Ordover, pp. 235-50. Norwood, N.J.: Ablex Publishing.

Sharkey, William, and David Sibley. 1985. "Applications of Public Utility Pricing Theory to BOC Pricing Issues." Bell Communications Research, Discussion Paper #11, (December) Morristown, N.J.

Skowronek, Stephen. 1982. *Building a New American State: The Expansion of National Administrative Capacities, 1877-1920*, Cambridge: Cambridge University Press.

Smith, Lincoln. 1978. "State Utility Commissions—1978," *Public Utilities Fortnightly* (16 February): 9–15.

Smith, Lincoln. 1984. "Regulatory Commissions in 1984—Are the Dice Loaded?" *Public Utilities Fortnightly* (10 May): 15–19.

Stigler, George J. 1971. "The Theory of Economic Regulation." *Bell Journal of Economics and Management Science* 2 (Spring): 3–21.

Stone, Alan. 1989. *Wrong Number: The Breakup of AT&T.* New York: Basic Books.

Taylor, William. 1986. "Federal and State Issues in Non-Traffic Sensitive Cost Recovery." Bell Communications Research. Draft, prepared for Forum on Telecommunications Deregulation, Tucson, Arizona, June 5-6.

Telecommunications Reports. 1986–1987. Capital Publishing Inc.

Telematics, The National Journal of Communications Business and Regulation. 1987 (January–May). Prentice Hall Law and Business.

Temin, Peter, with Louis Galambos. 1987. *The Fall of the Bell System.* Cambridge: Cambridge University Press.

Teske, Paul. 1987. "State Telecommunications Regulation: Assessing Issues and Options in the Midst of Changing Circumstances." Report of an Aspen Institute Conference, August 11–15, Aspen, Colorado.

Tuck-Jenkins, Linda, and Catharine A. Milmore. 1986. "Federal and State Regulations and Their Compatability with the New Environment in Telecommunications: The Virginia Experience." Paper presented to the Forum on Telecommunications Deregulation, Tucson, Arizona, June 5-6.

Ubis, Susan. 1986. "Illinois Law Carves path toward Local Exchange Competition." *Telephony Magazine,* 21 April: 85–97.

Vietor, Richard, and Dekkers Davidson. 1985. "Economics and Politics of Deregulation." *Journal of Policy Analysis and Management* 5, no. 1: 3–22.

Vietor, Richard, and Davis Dyer, editors. 1986. *Telecommunications in Transition: Managing Business and Regulatory Change,* Boston: Harvard Business School Press.

von Auw, Alvin. 1983. *Heritage and Destiny: Reflections on the Bell System in Transition.* New York: Praeger.

Walker, Jack. 1969. "The Diffusion of Innovation Among American States." *American Political Science Review* (September): 880–99.

Weingast, Barry, and Mark Moran. 1983. "Bureaucratic Discretion or Congressional Control? Regulatory Policymaking by the Federal Trade Commission." *Journal of Political Economy* 91, no. 5: 765–800.

Weingast, Barry, Mark Moran, and Randall Calvert. 1987. "Congressional Influence over Policy-making: The Case of the FTC." In *Congress: Structure and Policy,* edited by Mathew McCubbins and Terry Sullivan, pp. 493–521. Cambridge: Cambridge University Press.

Wenders, John. 1987. *The Economics of Telecommunications.* Cambridge, Mass.: Ballinger.

Wildavsky, Aaron. 1987. "Choosing Preferences by Constructing Institutions: A Cultural Theory of Preference Formation." *American Political Science Review* (March) 81.

Willig, Robert. 1979. "The Theory of Network Access Pricing." In *Issues in Public Utility Regulation*, edited by Harry Trebing, pp. 109-52. Michigan State University, East Lansing, Michigan.

Wilson, James Q. 1974. "The Politics of Regulation," in *Social Responsibility and the Business Predicament*, edited by James McKie, pp. 135-168. Washington, D.C.: Brookings Institution.

Wilson, James Q. 1980. *The Politics of Regulation*. New York: Basic Books.

Wilson, James Q. 1985. "Neglected Areas of Research on Regulation." In *Regulatory Policy and the Social Sciences*, edited by Roger Noll, pp. 357-363. Berkeley: University of California Press.

Wilson, John W. 1983. "Telephone Access Costs and Rates." *Public Utilities Fortnightly* (15 September): 18-25.

Wright, Gerald, Robert Erikson, and John McIver. 1987. "State Political Culture and Public Opinion." *American Political Science Review* (September): Vol. 81, no. 3: pp. 797-814.

INDEX

Above 890 decision (FCC), 3
ACC. *See* Arizona Corporation
 Commission
Access loop costs, 35, 36, 37;
 analysis of state decisions and, 64,
 68-69, 80, 83; in Illinois, 108; state
 policy choices and, 129; U S West
 and, 115
Access loops, 31-32
American Petroleum Institute, 10
American Telephone and Telegraph
 (AT&T): antitrust case in 1982,
 viii; divestiture and, 8; history of,
 2-5; Illinois Bell and, 108;
 Nebraska and, 119; repricing and,
 60
Antitrust suit, AT&T, viii, 4
Apportioning costs, 4
Arizona, 120-22
Arizona Corporation Commission
 (ACC), 120
Association of Data Communica-
 tions Users, 10
AT&T. *See* American Telephone and
 Telegraph
Average residential consumer, 52-55

Baby Bells, 5
Barbour, George, 93
Baumol, William, 94
Bell, Alexander Graham, 1
Bell Atlantic, 96
Bell Company, 1-2
Bell Labs, 5
Bell Operating Companies (BOCs),
 5, 8
Board of Public Utilities,
 New Jersey, 93-96
Board-to-board pricing, 2-3, 31, 34
BOCs. *See* Bell Operating Companies

Bradford, Peter, 100
Bureau of Labor Statistics 1984
 Consumer Expenditure Survey,
 45
Burke, Edward, 48, 136
Bypass, 37-38; estimated possible
 costs of, 47; Illinois and, 106;
 interest groups hypotheses and,
 126; New Jersey and, 96-98, 100;
 New York and, 92, 96-98; private
 line connections and, 47

Cable television, 20, 128; analysis of
 state decisions and, 67-68;
 penetration of in New York and
 New Jersey, 89; U S West and, 114
CALCs. *See* Customer access line
 charges, 40
Call externality, 34
Calling patterns, 68
Capture/ideology framework
 (Harvard School), 25-26, 67
CarterPhone decision (FCC), 3
CCTU. *See* Committee of Corporate
 Telecommunications Users
Centrex, 15, 138-9n. 9
Chicago School, 19, 125
Citicorp, 60
Committee of Corporate
 Telecommunications Users
 (CCTU), 10, 58
Communications Act (1934), 2
Communications Workers of
 America, 121
Competitive entry decisions, 76-80;
 consumer advocacy and, 127-28;
 elected commissioners and, 130;
 Idaho and, 123; Illinois and, 105-
 8; interest groups and, 128; legisla-
 tive party control and, 132;

157